D1050480

The Sleeping Juror

The Sleeping Juror

& Other Baldwin County Courtroom Tales and History

Samuel N. Crosby

Alabama Law Foundation
2002

Alabama Law Foundation, Inc.
Post Office Box 671
Montgomery, Alabama 36101-0671

For information on ordering additional copies of this book,
call the Alabama Law Foundation at 1-800-354-6154
or see www.alfinc.org

The Sleeping Juror
& Other Baldwin County Courtroom Tales and History

Library of Congress Control Number: 2002111103
ISBN 0-9717776-0-8

Manufactured in the United States of America

The text of this book is composed in11/14 Book Antiqua,
with the display set in CG Omega

Design and composition by
Suzanne S. Barnhill, Words into Type

Cover design by MaryLou Hyland

Publishing assistance by Sonny Brewer
Over the Transom Publishing Company
Fairhope, Alabama

First Edition 2002

10 9 8 7 6 5 4 3 2 1

Acknowledgments

The publication of this book was made possible through the generous contributions of the following firms to the Alabama Law Foundation:

AmSouth Bank
Armbrecht, Jackson, L.L.P.
Blackburn and Connor, P.C.
Carr, Allison, Pugh, Howard, Oliver & Sisson, P.C.
Chason & Chason, P.C.
Citrin & McGlothren, P.C.
Coale, Dukes, Kirkpatrick & Crowley, P.C.
Cunningham, Bounds, Yance, Crowder & Brown, L.L.C.
Daniell, Upton, Perry & Morris, P.C.
Irby & Heard, P.C.
Stone, Granade & Crosby, P.C.
The Hatchett Foundation
Wilkins, Bankester, Biles & Wynne, P.A.
Wills & Simon

The Alabama Law Foundation is a nonprofit charitable entity affiliated with the Alabama State Bar Association. All sales proceeds will be used for its charitable purposes, which include funding Kid's Chance (a scholarship fund for children of Alabama workers who have been killed or totally disabled in on-the-job accidents) and providing legal services to indigent Alabama citizens.

What does the Lord require of you?
To do justice, love mercy and walk
humbly with your God.

Micah 6:8

Foreword

In *The Sleeping Juror,* Sam Crosby provides not only an invaluable historical record of the courts of Baldwin County, Alabama, but a tale full of hilarious antics that have taken place in those courts.

The judges and attorneys, both famous and infamous, who have made their appearances in Baldwin County over the years are in evidence here, making Crosby's well-researched account a must-read for local history buffs and collectors of courtroom humor both in the county and throughout the state.

The author's respect for the court system and the legal profession is clear on every page. His writing reflects not only his keen sense of humor but, more important, his true love of people and his full understanding of human nature. The ultimate value of this book is that it could serve as the saga of any legal system in any county in any state in the country.

The fact that all sales proceeds will be used by the Alabama Law Foundation to provide scholarships to Alabama students and to provide legal services to indigent Alabama citizens makes this work a particularly good investment for any reader.

MORRIS DEES

Table of Contents

Preface

During my first year in the practice of law in Baldwin County, two very drunk men wandered in off the street to see me. One of the two men was slightly more sober than the other and was holding him up to keep him conscious despite his inebriated state. The two staggered into my office and sat down, almost missing the chairs. More than a bit puzzled, I asked, "What can I do for you?"

The more sober of the two, who was still holding his friend up so he wouldn't fall face down on our floor, replied, "He wanna make a will and leave ever'thin' to me."

In spite of myself, I laughed loudly, and with the tears of laughter in my eyes, explained why I could not help them and ushered them out the door. After these men left, I realized I should record other similar events I had either heard about or experienced while practicing law.

A few years later, while I was serving as the municipal judge for the Town of Loxley, I had a case that encouraged me to continue to record humorous incidents. In the case, the defendant was charged with driving his vehicle 55 miles per hour in a 35-mile-per-hour speed zone. He filed a written motion to dismiss the case with the Court clerk. As grounds for the motion, he pled that the Town of Loxley, Alabama, had no personal jurisdiction over him because he was "an interplanetary traveler from Mars and therefore was not subject to the laws of the planet Earth."

The inspiration for the historical parts of this book came when I discovered the following eulogy to a deceased local attorney while perusing the Baldwin County Circuit Court minutes from an April 20, 1869, court term:

> The members of the Bar in attendance on the Spring Term of the Circuit Court of Baldwin County have learned

with profound sadness of the recent death of John Hall, Esq., long associated as a lawyer with the administration of public justice in this County. Mr. Hall's name as an advocate and attorney appears on the docket of this court for more than thirty years past and in all that time and under the various trials of a position involving always the interests of life, liberty, character or property he has sustained the reputation of an able lawyer, a wise counselor, an unselfish and honest man. His friends and his companions at the Bar refer to this record of his public life with pride and satisfaction, and as a memorial of our respect for his memory the following Resolutions are adopted:

First: That we cherish in grateful remembrance the virtues of our deceased brother, his generous and warm sympathies in social life, the firm integrity of his character in all his professional and personal relations, the clearness of his mind and the soundness of his judgment and the fidelity of his attention, in all matters and causes committed to his charge.

Second: That while we bow in humble submission to that Providence which under painful circumstances, hath removed him from our social and professional intercourse forever, we will remember with gratitude that he hath been permitted for so long a time to illustrate the character of an upright and faithful lawyer and to preserve without spot or blemish, his reputation for truth, honor, integrity and charity.

Third: That we tender to the family and relatives of our deceased friend, our hearty sympathy in their affliction and in their sorrow.

Fourth: That as a permanent evidence of our appreciation of the high and noble qualities of Mr. Hall's character, the Presiding Judge of this Court be requested to have these proceedings entered in the minutes of the Court where they may remain as a part of the public records of this County.

The Honorable John Elliott, the Judge presiding, allowed the motion and in doing so remarked as follows:

> Mr. Hall, if somewhat reserved in his manner, was a very genial, kind-hearted man of unsullied honor and integrity.
>
> He did not possess brilliant or showy talents but in his opinions and arguments he exhibited the qualities of clear, sound and well directed reasoning powers.
>
> Although not a man of learning strictly speaking, he seemed to be thoroughly inbred with the principles of law, both natural and municipal.
>
> I heartily concur in the sentiments expressed in the resolutions, and will direct, that they be spread upon the records of the Court as a memorial of the worth and virtues of our departed brother.

The work on this book was completed in 2001, which was the 190th Anniversary of Baldwin County's First Superior Court term and the 100th Anniversary of the relocation of the county seat from Daphne to Bay Minette.

The production of this book has been a cooperative effort. A debt of gratitude is owed by me to the following people as well as many others:

Suzanne S. Barnhill
Dan Blackburn
Shirley Bolton
Sonny Brewer
Jean Burt
Charolette Burton
Doyle Byrd
George Byrne
Charlotte Cabaniss
Charles Carr
Bill Carrigan
Allan Chason
Andy Citrin
Harwell Coale, Jr.
Jonathan Coleman
Ann Crosby
Cason Crosby
Eleanor McMillan Crosby
Sam Crosby, Jr.
Tracy Daniel
Morris Dees
Maura Dismuke
Rev. Thack Dyson
Bill Goodloe
Fred Granade
Winston Groom
Susan Hawkins
Sam Irby

John Lewis
Regina Mandrell
André Mitchell
Andrew Mullek
Mary Murchison
Nall Printing
Terri A. Nobles
Bonnie Norton
Barbara Rhodes
Mike Shipler
David Simon
James D. Smith
Norborne C. Stone, Jr.
David Wirtes
Marion Wynne

1

History: Early Baldwin County

The Origin

Baldwin County was originally created as part of the Mississippi Territory before Alabama was even recognized as a state. Over the years the original lines have been redrawn time and time again—generally cutting land away from the County and adding it to others such as Washington, Mobile, Monroe, and Escambia Counties. Despite all this, Baldwin still remains Alabama's largest county, with over 1600 square miles, which makes it larger than the state of Rhode Island.[1] Baldwin County has one of the richest legal heritages in the state, and the purpose of this book is to preserve this legal heritage and some of its humorous courtroom lore.

The Name of Baldwin

The original citizens of Baldwin County, many of whom came from Georgia, named the county after a Georgian, Abraham Baldwin.

Abraham Baldwin was born on November 22, 1754, in North Guilford, Connecticut. Baldwin's father was a blacksmith and a principal citizen of the town. Baldwin entered Yale College in 1768 at the age of fourteen and, after graduation, tutored at Yale, studied theology, and became a chaplain. He served as a chaplain in George Washington's Continental Army during the Revolutionary War.

[1]Kay Nuzum, *A History of Baldwin County* (Bay Minette, AL: Baldwin Times, 1990), pp. 55–56.

Abraham Baldwin[2]

Baldwin later turned to the study of law and was admitted to the Connecticut bar at the age of twenty-nine. In 1783 he moved to Georgia, where he opened a law office.

[2]Original portrait by Charles Frederick Naegele, "Abraham Baldwin," oil on canvas, used by permission of the Georgia Museum of Art, University of Georgia, Gift of F. Phinizy Calhoun.

In 1784, the Georgia legislature made Baldwin a trustee of a contemplated state university. In 1785, the Georgia legislature adopted a charter to establish the University of Georgia. Baldwin became the first president of the University of Georgia in 1786.

Also in 1786, Abraham Baldwin was selected as a state delegate to the Constitutional Convention at Philadelphia. When Baldwin came to Philadelphia in 1787, he was the leader of the Georgia delegation. He played a key role in resolving the conflict between the large and small states over the question of proportional representation and equal representation in the Congress. He was also a signer of the U.S. Constitution.

Earlier, in 1784, Abraham Baldwin had been elected a member of the Georgia legislature. He was selected in 1785 as one of the representatives from the State of Georgia to the Confederation Congress. He served in the Confederation Congress until he was elected to the House of Representatives in the First Congress of the United States under the new Constitution. Baldwin served in the U.S. House of Representatives until 1799 when he was elected to the Senate. He remained a senator until his death in 1807 at age fifty-three. He is buried in the Rock Creek Cemetery in Washington, D.C.

Baldwin County was named for Abraham Baldwin by some of the earliest settlers, who thought he was a great leader. Baldwin County was created December 21, 1809, two years after Baldwin's death. Abraham Baldwin never visited Baldwin County.[3]

First Term of Court

The first term of the Baldwin County Superior Court was held on March 4, 1811, at McIntosh Bluff. The Honorable Harry Toulmin presided and the Court records reflect the following:

[3] Ellis Merton Coulter, *Abraham Baldwin: Patriot, Educator and Founding Father* (Clearwater, FL: Vandamere Press, 1987); and Jethro K. Lieberman, *The Enduring Constitution: A Bicentennial Perspective* (St. Paul, MN: West Publishing Co., 1987). Thanks to Sam Irby for contributing the section on Abraham Baldwin.

Superior Court of Baldwin County March 4, 1811. Judge Toulmin appeared at the place appointed by the commissioners for the site of the Court House of Baldwin County and opened court and the clerk not appearing, upon being called....

Rodin H. Gilmer, Joseph P. Kennedy, Joseph Carson, Francis McHenry and Edmund P. Gaines were severally sworn and admitted as counselors & attorneys at Law—and Lemuel Henry & Matthew D. Wilson were also sworn and admitted as counselors & attorneys at Law—On motion of F. D. McHenry, no commissioned Clerk appearing, that the proceedings be continued until tomorrow morning—the same is overruled—Ordered that Lemuel Henry, R. H. Gilmer, J. P. Kennedy, Joseph Carson and Matthew D. Wilson be requested to Report to this Court a system of Rules of Practice to be observed therein.[4]

First County Seat

Approximately nine months after the first term of Court, the following act was passed by the Alabama legislature establishing the town of Dumfries at McIntosh Bluff as the county seat of Baldwin County:

An act to establish a town in Baldwin County, by the name of Dumfries, passed on December 13, 1811. Be It Enacted by the Legislative Council and the Representatives of the Alabama Territory in general assembly convened, that there shall be established a town, to be called by the name of Dumfries, on the lands of Joseph Polaskie Kennedy; it shall be the duty of the proprietor to have recorded in the clerk's office of the County of Baldwin a plan of said town, within six months after the passage of the act.

And be it further enacted that the said proprietor may appoint a trustee or trustees to sell, lease or otherwise

[4]Nuzum, *History of Baldwin County,* p. 163.

dispose of the lots in said town, and due conveyances make for the same.

Court Stories: In The Courtroom

Many amusing tales have resulted from statements made in local courtrooms.

In about 1910 Frank Stone represented an attractive young female chiropractor who moved to Bay Minette. The elderly doctors in town had her prosecuted for practicing medicine without a license because they were losing patients to her. Frank Stone, during his examination of each of the old doctors, asked the following questions about patients of theirs whom he knew were deceased.

Q Doctor, was Mr. Brown a patient of yours?
A Yes.
Q Where is he now?
A He's dead.
Q Doctor, was Mr. Jones a patient of yours?
A Yes.
Q Where is he now?
A He's dead.

In his closing argument, Frank Stone asked the jury if they "would rather be practiced to death by these old fogies or rubbed to death by this good-looking young woman?" The amused jury acquitted the woman of the charges.

~

A number of years ago, Judge Telfair Mashburn repeatedly handled cases filed by a particular woman seeking child support from her ex-husband. Her ex-husband had a good job, but continued to fail to make his child support payments.

At the last of the several non-support hearings, a frustrated Judge Mashburn angrily told the ex-husband, "I'm tired of you repeatedly not doing what you are supposed to do. I am going to see to it that your ex-wife gets four hundred dollars per month!"

The confused man remarked, "Thank you very much for that, Judge. I'll try to chip in a little money to her myself."

~

Louis E. Braswell recounted the following story about Taylor D. ("Red") Wilkins, Jr., who is a fine trial lawyer and a colorful character:

> In a closing argument before a jury, Red Wilkins was characteristically emphatic about the truthfulness of the points made on behalf of his client. To underscore the truthfulness dramatically, Red approached the jury, took a mechanical pencil from his pocket and held the pencil near his throat. Then Red looked the jury in the eye, jerked the pencil across his neck in a throat-slitting maneuver, and said, "If I am not telling the truth, you can slit my 'thoat.'"
>
> The argument seemed to work well, and Red continued making some more points. But then Bayless Biles, Red's partner, had to intervene. Bayless pulled Red's sleeve, finally diverted Red's attention briefly away from the closing argument, and in a stage whisper that coincided with something the jury was already beginning to notice said, 'Red, your throat is bleeding.' Apparently, the pocket clip on the pencil had nicked or 'sliced' Red's throat during his dramatic gesture.

~

Another story involved a Baldwin County man who was arrested in Mobile by a beautiful undercover female police officer who was disguised as a prostitute. The man unsuccessfully attempted to raise the defense of entrapment at his trial. He was convicted, and prior to the sentencing the judge asked if there was anything he had to say for himself before the sentence of law was passed upon him. The defendant stated, "Well, Judge, they caught me this time, and I'll tell you, that was the best-looking woman I've ever seen. If they use the same bait in the same trap, they'll probably catch me again."

~

While Julian "Buddy" Brackin was serving as a municipal judge, he tried one case involving a man who, at midnight, had intentionally driven his truck into the side of a building owned by a religious cult. The man pled guilty to the charge and the following exchange occurred prior to sentencing:

Q Why on earth did you intentionally drive your truck into that building in the middle of the night?
A Your Honor, the people in that cult started coming to my house every night trying to recruit my wife and she finally fell subject to their influence.
Q That still does not explain your driving into that building.
A On the night I committed the crime, I was so angry with the people in the cult that I was driving my truck around until midnight. Finally, I just lost control and I rammed my truck into their building.
Q Don't you know you could have killed somebody?
A Judge, I figured they were probably all over at my house.

~

One afternoon, Buddy Brackin was involved in a heated motion argument in Circuit Court before Judge Charles Partin. During the argument, Buddy got so upset with the other lawyer that he slammed his hand down on the counsel table and shouted, "Judge, if what that other lawyer is saying is true, then I'm a monkey!"

Judge Partin looked down from the bench, slowly grinned from ear to ear, and said absolutely nothing.

~

Robert T. Cunningham, Jr. contributed the following story:

As a young lawyer not many years at the bar, I was trying a case in Baldwin County, a jurisdiction somewhat feared by young Mobile lawyers. The case was being tried before the Honorable Wilson Hayes, a newly elected circuit judge. I had been a lawyer for only a few years, but I had been a lawyer a lot longer than Judge Hayes had been a judge. The trial of this automobile accident case was one of his first cases as a judge. Much of his experience had been defending cases. I was questioning a state trooper when, much to my surprise Judge Hayes, forgetting he was a judge and thinking he was a defense lawyer, slapped the bench, leaned over, and said "I object!" I did the only thing I could do. I looked him in the eye, gritted my teeth and said "Overruled!" The witness answered the question, the jury looked befuddled, and the trial continued with no further objections from the judge.

~

A number of years ago, as I sat in the Circuit Court of Baldwin County, I overheard the following exchange. After the entry of a guilty plea to a theft charge, Judge Harry Wilters asked the defendant, "Do you have any prior offenses?"

The defendant replied, "No sir, I ain't never stole this much."

Judge Wilters asked again, "What other offenses have you committed?"

The defendant said, "Nothing serious!"

Judge Wilters asked, "What do you call serious?"

The defendant defensively replied, "Well, I ain't never murdered nobody."

~

While serving as a municipal judge, John E. Chason tried a man charged with driving under the influence of alcohol. The man had been found asleep at the wheel of his car, which was parked in the middle of a busy street. The man's defense was that, although he had drunk one beer, the reason he fell asleep at the wheel was that he had to drive his brother-in-law home. He said his brother-in-law is the most boring person he has ever known and never stopped talking during the entire trip. After his brother-in-law got out of the car, the defendant was so bored he fell asleep at the wheel of his car while it was parked in front of his brother-in-law's house.

~

The following story about a criminal trial judge was contributed by Mr. Claude Bagge of Bon Secour.

> The judge asked a criminal defendant during an arraignment, "What is your name?"
>
> The defendant answered, "My name is Joshua."
>
> The judge jokingly replied, "Are you the one who made the sun stand still?"
>
> The defendant answered, "No sir, I'm the one who made the moon shine."

~

Once L. D. Owen, III was representing a man in a divorce case. Kenneth Cooper, who was one of the oldest practicing attorneys at that time in Baldwin County, was representing the wife. One of the issues in the case was a complaint by the wife that the husband should reimburse her for a dental bill which was incurred because the husband had struck her and broken her tooth.

On cross examination, Attorney Cooper asked the man if he had hit and injured his wife. The man readily admitted that he had done so. Then Mr. Cooper asked the man if he was willing to pay the $500 dental bill. The man shook his head and responded "No!"

Mr. Cooper continued and simply asked "Why?"

The courtroom became very quiet and the man replied, "because it was a used tooth." Needless to say, the man was ordered to pay the dental bill.

~

In one case, Harry Wilters and Tolbert Brantley were defending a man charged with the fish and game violation of "telephoning" fish. Kenneth Cooper was prosecuting the case, and in his cross-examination he asked, "You were telephoning fish off the east bank of that river weren't you?"

The defendant answered, "No!" Then, without thinking, he added, "It was off the other bank." In spite of this answer, the jury acquitted the defendant, to the dismay of everyone in the courtroom, especially Harry Wilters and Tolbert Brantley.

~

Judge Michael Zoghby of Mobile once had a man in his court who became furious with the judge after being sentenced for a crime. The irate man shouted at the judge, "You are a jackass."

Judge Zoghby said, "I find you in contempt of court and sentence you to three days in the county jail for that remark."

The man responded, "I am very sorry for the outburst, Judge. I just didn't know you could get three days in jail for calling a judge a jackass, and I apologize. Tell me Judge, what is the sentence for calling a jackass 'Judge'?"

Judge Zoghby responded there is no sentence for that.

The man replied, "Thank you, Judge."

~

A defense lawyer was once defending a man charged with murder in a stabbing death that occurred late at night. The only eyewitness to the incident was an old woman from the country, and the defense lawyer decided to try to bear down on her in an attempt to discredit her testimony. The following exchange occurred.

Q This night of the stabbing was a dark night, wasn't it, Mrs. Jones?"

A Yes, sir, it was.

Q You can't see at all in the dark can you, Mrs. Jones?

A Not very well, sir.

Q You can't see thirty feet or twenty feet or ten feet or even five feet in the dark, can you, Mrs. Jones? Just how far can you see in the dark?

To the shock of the defense lawyer, the witness answered, "I can see the moon, sir, how far is that?"

~

Every lawyer has had to try to gracefully recover from such an answer. Once, while trying a case, a client informed me that he didn't have a job and absolutely could not pay the funds at issue. Several days prior to the trial, however, he had obtained employment without my knowledge. I tried to emphasize during the trial that he was destitute. While my client was on the stand and after his testimony, the circuit judge asked me if he had a job. I said "No" at precisely the same time my client answered "Yes." I never quite recovered from this exchange during the rest of the trial.

~

All lawyers ask questions of witnesses that are difficult to understand and answer. Taylor "Red" Wilkins, Jr. is one local lawyer whom I have heard ask such questions. The following question asked by him of a witness is taken from the transcript of a 1997 trial in which Mr. Wilkins' law firm and our law firm participated.

> Now, is it—have you already testified here on cross-examination today, and is it your opinion and do you agree with Mr. Harry Riddick when he wrote this memorandum to the partnership that the partnership agreement is silent as with respect to if another partner violates the partnership agreement and that under the partnership agreement he said there wasn't— in his opinion as a partnership lawyer, they didn't even have a right to expel the offending partner and that the purchase in book value exists only if a partner withdraws, he's talking about this partnership agreement, or dies or becomes permanently disabled. And then he underlines here, therefore, neither the partnership or any person has any right—I know I read slow and talk slow, and you can—y'all are probably way ahead of me seeing it already—that you can't purchase at book value unless an agreement is reached. Did you understand that?

Court Stories: Lawyer Fees

Jimmy Lindsey of Bay Minette contributed the following story involving a criminal defendant who had no funds with which to employ an attorney.

The local attorney who was employed required that the defendant sign a promissory note and mortgage to secure payment of his fee. The defendant was charged with murder and the attorney successfully raised the insanity defense and obtained an acquittal for his client.

When the attorney mentioned collecting his fee after the case was concluded, the defendant remarked, "If I was insane at the time I committed the offense, how could I have been sane when I signed the promissory note and mortgage securing payment of your fee?"

~

A Baldwin County attorney handled a legal matter for a widow. After receiving the bill, the widow called the attorney and complained to him about the amount of the charges.

The attorney was confident that the charges were reasonable and suggested to the widow that they submit the amount of the bill to four local attorneys to obtain their opinions regarding the reasonableness of the bill.

The widow's response was, "I don't want to do that. I want to submit the bill to four widows and ask them whether they think the charges are reasonable."

~

One local criminal defense lawyer tells his clients the following when he gets ready to quote his fee: "I'm the type of person who can only worry about one thing at a time. I can either worry about getting paid by you or worry about your case. What would you rather have me do?"

The same criminal defense lawyer says he always keeps two fundamental tenets in mind in his practice. The first is he only worries about the *big* things in the practice of law, and the second is that nothing is big.

2

History: Early Legal Figures

Harry Toulmin

Baldwin County's first legal system was to a great degree a reflection of its first judge, Harry Toulmin, who was one of the most important figures in our county's history.

Judge Toulmin's descendant, the late Harry T. Toulmin of Daphne, Alabama, graciously allowed me to reprint excerpts from the following report he presented about his ancestor to the Baldwin County Historical Society:

> Judge Harry Toulmin was born in Taunton, England, on April 7, 1766, and died at Washington Courthouse, Alabama, on November 11, 1823. The vast Tombigbee District of the Mississippi Territory (later the Alabama Territory) where he served as a federal judge included Baldwin County. The seat of justice where Toulmin first held court was at McIntosh Bluff, and this courthouse became the first seat of government of Baldwin County. Harry Toulmin was also the delegate from Baldwin County to the 1819 Alabama State Constitutional Convention.

Harry Toulmin

> On May 14, 1793, with his wife and four small children, Harry Toulmin sailed from Bristol on the American ship *Sisters Bound for Norfolk.*

Harry Toulmin served as President of Transylvania College in Lexington, Kentucky, but in April 1796 Toulmin resigned from Transylvania, stating low salary and impermanence of the position as the reasons. A few weeks later he was appointed Secretary of State of Kentucky by Governor James Garrard, a Jeffersonian Republican of some prominence. In 1798, while Toulmin was Secretary of State, he signed the famed Kentucky Resolutions written by Thomas Jefferson.

During this political interlude as Secretary of State Toulmin busied himself in his spare hours with remunerative efforts which ranged from selling sets of Blackstone's *Commentaries* to breeding racehorses. One major outside interest stood him in good stead during his later years. He began to study and research extensively, first in the laws of the State of Kentucky and later in the laws of the new United States.

On November 22, 1804, President Jefferson appointed Harry Toulmin Judge of the Superior Court in the Tombigbee District (officially the Washington District) of the Mississippi Territory.

The Tombigbee District was one of the wildest and least populous areas of the old southwest frontier of the new United States. It comprised the vast area later incorporated into the State of Alabama. The greatest concentration of settlement was on the lower Tombigbee, particularly in the vicinity of Fort Stoddert. The most respectable and law-abiding citizens lived around Boatyard Lake and in the Tensaw settlements.

Toulmin's official duties as a federal judge consisted of presiding over the territorial district court, but he soon discovered that the chief federal civil official in a vast frontier wilderness confronted a myriad of unspecified responsibilities. He became at once local diplomat and reporter to Washington and Natchez, federal representative, postmaster, chief legal official, symbol of law and order, and keeper of the peace.

On December 10, 1817, Mississippi became a state. Simultaneously, Alabama became a separate territory with its seat of government at St. Stephens. President James Monroe appointed William Wyatt Bibb as Governor of the Alabama Territory and Harry Toulmin's tenure as judge continued.

By act of March 2, 1819, Congress directed the election of delegates to a constitutional convention of state government for the people within the Alabama Territory. Baldwin County was permitted one representative and chose Harry Toulmin as its delegate. Harry Toulmin was an articulate spokesman for the interests of South Alabama. The Alabama Constitution was confirmed by joint resolution of Congress on December 14, 1819, and Alabama became a state on that date.

Harry Toulmin's position as territorial judge ceased to exist when the State's first General Assembly elected five circuit court judges. Under the new State Constitution these judges, sitting together, would also compose the state's Supreme Court. For judge of the first judicial circuit, Abner Lipscomb defeated Harry Toulmin 63 to 5.

By 1821, when the third annual session of the legislature met at Cahawba, the need for a digest of laws of the State (including the predecessor laws of the Territory) had become acute. Having failed to make the justices of the Supreme Court prepare the digest, the Assembly elected Harry Toulmin to do this important work. By devoting himself assiduously to the task, Toulmin was able to submit his digest the following year to the fourth annual session of the Assembly.

A joint committee which examined Toulmin's manuscript reported that the statute laws had been digested with accuracy, correctness, and much ability, and that the arrangement was good, being far superior to the 1816 *Mississippi Digest* (by Turner) which it would supplant. A bill was reported by the committee whereby the State accepted the digest and paid Toulmin for his services.

Unfortunately, Alabama's treasury was low, and the assemblymen haggled about the price. Waiting in Cahawba for action, Toulmin was sick and knew he would soon die; nevertheless he registered his concern for his rights. Knowing of the debate on December 22, 1822, the ailing judge dispatched this letter to the Assembly:

"The undersigned has known from long experience what are the labor and the expenses of attending seven circuit courts twice a year and discharging the duties not only of a Territorial but of a Federal judge; he can say with confidence that neither the mental exertion nor the personal expense (even including clerk hire) has been equal to that of preparing the digest now presented to the Legislature.

"It was necessary that the compiler...attend at the present session about four weeks, in order to facilitate an examination of the digest. He conceives therefore that his traveling expenses (having been obliged to bring a wagon for conveying the digest and original acts of the Legislature on which the digest is formed) together with attendance cannot be estimated at less than two hundred and sixty-four dollars.

"His clerk hire and paper have cost him about two hundred fifty dollars. His labor for one year, taking that of a circuit judge as a criterion, is worth seventeen hundred and fifty dollars (total twenty-two hundred and sixty four dollars).

"The compiler of the [Turner] digest now in use had before him the digest of 1807 and of nine subsequent sessions some of which were very short. An appropriation was made to him of $1,000 in 1816 before the work was completed. What appropriations were made afterwards is not known. The present digest will contain the acts of sixteen sessions besides those of the digest of 1807. If it be supposed that Mr. Turner received no more than $1,000 for the chaos he created, it will surely be a subject of a very rational investigation what sum, when a man has been paid $1,000 for mangling and murdering the laws, ought to be paid to anyone who has brought them to life again.

"...The undersigned has endeavored not only to gratify but to be useful to the public. He cannot receive for his services a less sum than about $2,000. If the General Assembly do not deem his services worthy of that compensation, he prays permission to withdraw his manuscript. He has labored incessantly and what he solicits is not from the generosity, but the justice of the General Assembly."

The Assembly finally authorized a payment of $1,500 to Toulmin—with the proviso that he prepare an index and superintend the printing of the book. Before his death, Toulmin prepared a table of contents for this most famous of Alabama law books, but he died at the age of fifty-seven before making the index.

Toulmin's Justice System

During his tenure on the bench, Judge Toulmin administered a vastly different justice system than our current system, based upon many statutes which have long since been repealed such as the following:

An Act To Prevent The Evil Practice of Dueling
Passed November 11, 1804

WHEREAS, from a false sense of honour, the inhuman, injurious, and detestable practice of dueling, has been too often and unhappily resorted to as a mode of adjusting or settling differences of small magnitude between individuals: AND WHEREAS, this barbarous and savage conduct has of late obtained a great degree of prevalence, to the destruction of the lives of some valuable members of society, and involving the feelings of others, who from principle, and respect for the laws of their country, will not engage in this pernicious practice: BE IT, THEREFORE, ENACTED BY THE LEGISLATIVE COUNCIL AND HOUSE OF REPRESENTATIVES OF THE MISSISSIPPI

TERRITORY, IN GENERAL ASSEMBLY CONVENED, AND IT IS HEREBY ENACTED BY THE AUTHORITY OF THE SAME: That from and after the passing of this act, if any person or persons shall deliver, offer, or send any challenge in writing, verbally, or otherwise, to fight a duel, or shall accept such challenge, or shall fight a duel, and neither of the parties be killed, or shall be the bearer of such challenge, knowing the same to be such, the person or persons so offending, their aiders, or abettors, and each of them, shall on conviction thereof, be fined in the sum of one thousand dollars, and be imprisoned twelve calendar months, and be rendered incapable of holding any office of honour, profit, or trust under the government of this territory, for and during the term of five years from the time of such conviction.

SEC. 2. AND BE IT FURTHER ENACTED, That if any person or persons residing or being in this territory shall promote, consort, plan or in any manner encourage the fighting of a duel between persons residing or being in this territory, whether the same duel be fought within this territory or elsewhere, such person or persons shall be subject to the pains and penalties prescribed in the preceding section of this act.

SEC. 3. AND BE IT FURTHER ENACTED, That if any person residing or being in this territory, do hereafter actually fight a duel, and either of the combatants be killed; the survivor, with such other person or persons who may have aided or assisted in the said duel, shall be deemed guilty of wilful murder, and on conviction thereof, shall suffer death.

Another example of a statute of that era addresses the welfare of the indigent:

An Act for the Settlement and Relief of the Poor

SEC. 1. BE IT ENACTED BY THE LEGISLATURE COUNCIL AND HOUSE OF REPRESENTATIVES OF THE MISSISSIPPI TERRITORY, That it shall be the duty of the justices of the county courts, in their respective counties, at their first courts, which shall be held after the passing of this act; and yearly thereafter to appoint one or more overseers of the poor in each captain's district, to serve for the term of one whole year, or until another district overseer shall be appointed: and any person so appointed, who shall refuse or neglect to serve as overseer of the poor, unless disqualified by age or infirmity, of which the justices shall judge, shall forfeit and pay fifty dollars, to be recovered with costs by action of debt in any court having competent jurisdiction, for the use of the county....

SEC. 2. AND BE IT FURTHER ENACTED, That it shall be the duty of the overseers of the poor, each in his respective district, to provide for the indigent, lame, blind, and others not able to maintain themselves; and may also provide houses, nurses and physicians, in such cases as they shall think necessary; the expenses of which shall be lawful for the overseers of the poor to contract with any person or persons for keeping, maintaining, and employing any or all such poor persons, and take the benefit of their work, labour, or service, towards their maintenance and support.

John Gaston Aikin And His Era

John Gaston Aikin

The second compilation of the laws of the State of Alabama was prepared by a Baldwin County attorney, John Gaston Aikin, of Stockton. He prepared *Aikin's Digest* in 1833, and compiled a second edition of his digest in 1836.

John Gaston Aikin was a native of Abbeville, South Carolina. He was the son of Robert Aikin, a native of Pennsylvania and a Whig soldier in the American Revolution. John Aikin was born November 29, 1803, and died November 29, 1865. He married Clarissa Amanda Kennedy, who was the daughter of Joshua and Susan Kennedy.

In order to place *Aikin's Digest* in its proper historical perspective, it is helpful to realize that it was published the same year that Davy Crockett was elected to Congress. Davy Crockett won a seat by defeating Adam Huntsman in 1833, before being defeated himself in 1836. The following writings of Davy Crockett illustrate that the politics of Aikin's time were not much different from the politics of the present:

Crockett's Rules for the Guidance of Politicians

> "Attend all public meetings," says I, "and get some friends to move that you take the chair; if you fail in this attempt, make a push to be appointed secretary; the proceedings of course will be published, and your name is introduced to the public. But should you fail in both undertakings, get two or three acquaintances, over a bottle of whiskey, to pass some resolutions, no matter on what subject; publish them even if you pay the printer—it will answer the purpose of breaking the ice, which is the main point in these matters. Intrigue until you are elected an officer of the militia; this is the second step towards promotion, and can be accomplished with ease, as I know

an instance of an election being advertised, and no one attending, the innkeeper at whose house it was to be held, having a military turn, elected himself colonel of his regiment." Says I, "You may not accomplish your ends with as little difficulty, but do not be discouraged—Rome wasn't built in a day.

"If your ambition or circumstances compel you to serve your country, and earn three dollars a day, by becoming a member of the legislature, you must first publicly avow that the constitution of the state is a shackle upon free and liberal legislation; and is, therefore, of as little use in the present enlightened age, as an old almanac of the year in which the instrument was framed. There is policy in this measure, for by making the constitution a mere dead letter, your headlong proceedings will be attributed to a bold and unshackled mind, whereas, it might otherwise be thought they arose from sheer mulish ignorance. 'The Government' has set the example in this attack upon the constitution of the United States, and who should fear to follow where 'the Government' leads?

"When the day of election approaches, visit your constituents far and wide. Treat liberally, and drink freely, in order to rise in their estimation, though you fall in your own. True, you may be called a drunken dog by some of the clean shirt and silk stocking gentry, but the real rough necks will style you a jovial fellow, their votes are certain, and frequently count double. Do all you can to appear to advantage in the eyes of the women. That's easily done—you have but to kiss and slabber their children, wipe their noses, and pat them on the head; this cannot fail to please their mothers, and you may rely on your business being done in that quarter.

"Promise all that is asked," said I, "and more if you can think of anything. Offer to build a bridge or a church, to divide a county, create a batch of new offices, make a turnpike, or anything they like. Promises cost nothing, therefore deny nobody who has a vote or sufficient influence to obtain one."

"Get up on all occasions, and sometimes on no occasion at all, and make long-winded speeches, though composed of nothing else than wind—talk of your devotion to your country, your modesty and disinterestedness, or on any such fanciful subject. Rail against taxes of all kinds, officeholders, and bad harvest weather; and wind up with a flourish about the heroes who fought and bled for our liberties in the times that tried men's souls. To be sure you run the risk of being considered a bladder of wind, or an empty barrel, but never mind that, you will find enough of the same fraternity to keep you in countenance."

"If any charity be going forward, be at the top of it, provided it is to be advertised publicly; if not, it isn't worth your while. None but a fool would place his candle under a bushel on such an occasion."

"These few directions," said I, "if properly attended to, will do your business; and when once elected, why a fig for the dirty children, the promises, the bridges, the churches, the taxes, the offices, and the subscriptions, for it is absolutely necessary to forget all these before you can become a thorough-going politician, and a patriot of the first water."[5]

Edmund Pendleton Gaines

A third important historical figure in the early years was Edmund Pendleton Gaines. He was admitted to the Baldwin County Bar at the initial term of Court on March 4, 1811, and he was the son-in-law of Judge Harry Toulmin. Edmund Gaines is given credit for the arrest of Aaron Burr on February 18, 1807, near McIntosh after

[5]David Crockett, *A Narrative of the Life of David Crockett of the State of Tennessee* (Philadelphia: John E. Potter Co., 1860), cited in B. A. Botkin, *A Treasury of Southern Folklore* (New York: Crown Publications, 1959), pp. 261–263.

Burr, a former vice-president of the United States, threatened to carve a new autonomous western empire from Spanish holdings on the Gulf of Mexico. Judge Toulmin issued the arrest warrant and Edmund Gaines, who was then with the regular army contingent at Fort Stoddert, arranged for Burr's transfer to Richmond for trial.

A Lawyer at Fort Mims

On August 30, 1813, under the leadership of William Weatherford, who was known as "Red Eagle," a group of Creek Indians attacked the settlement at Fort Mims in what is now North Baldwin County. The famous attack led to the death of settlers within the fort. Major Daniel Beasley, a lawyer, was in command of the fort. "Judge A. B. Meek spoke of fellow lawyer Beasley as "unflinchingly brave but vain, rash, inexperienced and overconfident."[6]

One of his descendants, Perry Zarr of Bay Minette, counters the allegations that Beasley was ill prepared for the attack by citing the statements of General Claiborne, his superior officer, who spoke of Beasley's bravery during the attack.

Court Stories: Out of the Mouths of Clients

Unexpected remarks and answers from clients have produced a wealth of humor.

An old story illustrates the dangers an attorney can encounter in asking too many questions on cross-examination. The attorney was defending a maiming case and his client was accused of having bitten off a man's ear. As he was questioning the only witness to the incident, he asked, "You didn't see this man (pointing to his client) bite the victim's ear off, did you?"

The witness answered, "No, sir, I did not."

[6]Information provided by Ms. Perry Zarr, Bay Minette, from General Claiborne's papers in the state archives of Alabama and Mississippi.

Instead of sitting down at this point with his case won, the defense attorney decided to ask one more question. "Then how could my client be guilty of this crime?"

The witness replied, "I saw him spit the man's ear out."

~

Bay Minette attorney David Simon contributed the following story. During one of David's first years in law practice he represented the husband in a divorce case. The wife alleged that the husband had an extramarital affair with another woman. To the surprise of David's client, the wife's lawyer called a private investigator to the witness stand to testify that he had observed the husband and another woman going into a bedroom at night on the second floor of an Atmore hotel. While the private investigator was testifying, the husband was elbowing David and saying, "You need to point out to the judge that he is lying." Before David began his cross-examination of the private investigator he whispered to his client, "Why do you say he is lying?" The man responded, "We were on the *first* floor, not the second floor."

~

One old story involved a bastardy proceeding during the pre-typewriter era, when all pleadings were written longhand. There was one insignificant error in a long petition to legitimate a child filed by a local lawyer, who was representing the child's father. The lawyer's client and the young child in question stopped by to talk with the judge after he had required the lawyer to reprepare the entire petition and correct the insignificant error before the Court would hear the matter. During their conversation, the judge said to the man, "Don't you see, if the petition is not correct, your child will not be legitimate. He is a technical bastard." The boy chimed in before his father could stop him, "Why, Judge, that's exactly what my daddy's lawyer said about you."

~

Baldwin County citizens have always been protective of their land. One story involved an old man who was watching part of a highway crew mow the grass on a right-of-way. A young fellow with the highway crew was about to drive the mower onto the old man's land. The old man ran out with a shotgun and said, "Don't come on my land!"

The young man said, "Sir, I just need to turn this mower around on a few feet of your land."

The old man said, "I told you, don't come on my land!"

The young fellow said, "But, sir!"

As he brandished his shotgun, the old man said, "I may not be able to keep you from coming on my land, but I can sure keep you from leaving!"

~

J. B. Blackburn was once appointed to represent a moonshiner. He told his client to find some alibi witnesses to testify at trial. Prior to meeting with these witnesses, Mr. Blackburn asked his client about their testimony. His client responded, "They're going to testify to whatever you want them to say. What do you want them to say?"

~

Fairhope attorney John Beck mentioned that during one of his first years in law practice, he was at a docket call in the district courtroom of Judge Robert Wilters. One of the cases Judge Wilters was to hear involved a man from Czechoslovakia who did not speak English. The courtroom was full of people, and at the point when Judge Wilters discovered the witness spoke only Czech, he announced, "Does anyone in here speak Czechoslovakian?" After a long period of silence, Judge Wilters turned to John Beck and said, "Mr. Beck, you are a Yankee. Why don't you see if you can understand him?"

~

In another case, John Beck represented a defendant who was charged with reckless endangerment in a trial before Julian

Brackin in the municipal court of Robertsdale, Alabama. John's client was accused of having hit the victim with a bush axe during a fight.

The cross-examination of John's client went in part as follows:

Q What did the victim say to you before the fight started?
A He said, "I know karate and you better not fight with me."
Q And how did you respond?
A I told him I know ka-bush axe and I ain't worried about karate.

~

After Jimmy Owen won his first big case he was so proud he decided he would go out and buy a brand new Cadillac. He proudly took it on a trip through North Baldwin County the day he bought it. On this trip he stopped and picked up an old country fellow who was hitchhiking. He asked the hitchhiker what he thought of his new car, hoping for the right reaction. The old fellow ran his hands gently over the seat and after carefully viewing the interior of the car he replied, "Why, Mr. Owen, I believe this is about the prettiest *Chevrolet* I have ever seen!"

~

J. B. Blackburn told me the following story about having a deed signed in the days when a separate acknowledgment of a wife's signature was required to insure that she signed the instrument voluntarily. Mr. Blackburn explained to the husband that he would have to "examine" his wife separately. The confused husband peeked in the window a number of times after he had left the room to insure that his wife had all her clothes on.

~

A local attorney recently told me the following story about a spoiled Baldwin County girl with a wise mother. The girl married a young man from Huntsville and after the wedding the couple moved to Huntsville. The girl telephoned her mother from Huntsville after her first quarrel with her new husband.

"Mama," she said, "we had a fight and I'm coming home."

The girl's mother replied, "Darling, I've got some news for you. You *are* home!

Court Stories: More Tales

As a politician, Judge Michael Zoghby of Mobile was careful not to offend voters while on the campaign trail. During one campaign, he stopped at a little country store with his brother. The proprietor of the store offered him a dip of snuff, asking, "Do you dip, Judge?"

Judge Zoghby looked at his brother, who was grinning from ear to ear wondering how he was going to get himself out of taking the snuff. The Judge thought a moment and said, "No, sir, I don't, but my brother here does."

~

Claude Bagge of Bon Secour contributed the following story he heard about a criminal trial that took place in a small town in the 1830s. After the close of the testimony the prosecutor made his argument to the jury. Before the defense attorney had an opportunity to argue, the judge turned to the jury and asked "Has the jury reached its verdict?"

The defense attorney stood up and objected "Wait, Your Honor, doesn't the defense get a chance to argue?"

The judge responded "No, that tends to confuse the jury."

~

In a recent local case the defendant clearly caused the automobile accident and was responsible for the damages. The defense lawyer's long-winded closing argument was an obvious attempt to confuse the jury about the facts. The frustrated plaintiff's lawyer, Bayless Biles, aptly opened his second argument by saying:

"When I was in law school, they taught us about that type of argument. They said if you have a good case on the law argue the law. If you have a good case on the facts, argue the facts. And if you don't have any case at all, argue confusion!"

~

Fred Granade once represented a woman in a divorce proceeding and received a telephone call at his office from her irate husband.

The husband told Fred that he was coming right down to our offices "to whip his a**."

Fred came rushing into my office and told me of his dilemma. We promptly went and told our senior partner, Charles Partin. Charles, who is 6'3" tall, and I decided we would stand out in the hall in front of Fred's office to help him if he needed it. The receptionist sent the irate husband down the hall. He was a little, skinny guy about five feet tall, who was wearing a baseball cap. Charles and I looked at the husband, grinned, and whispered to Fred, "We think you can handle him."

We were both chuckling as we stepped back into our own offices.

~

Allan Chason contributed the following excerpt from deposition testimony given several years ago in Baldwin County case.

The deponent was Craig Sheldon, a former columnist with the *Fairhope Courier.* The suit involved one of Mr. Sheldon's newspaper columns that featured conversations with a frog named Godfrey:

Q To your knowledge did he ever say that an article that you submitted contained language which he believed would be objectionable to the reader?

A (Mr. Sheldon): Uh-huh. In dealing with my dialogue, my dialogue comes about between myself and a frog. I am sure all of you have read the articles. I happen to have a frog that has lived in the world since the first millennium, which is always explained in the beginning of my columns.

Q The frog that you use is a tool, is he not?

A No, he is a friend.

Q Well, he is a friend that you use as a tool?
A He uses me, rather than me using him.
Q Well, you express viewpoints to the frog.
A No, he expresses his viewpoints; and quite often, if you read my column, you know that I argue with him.
Q Is your frog your alter ego?
A No, he is a frog.
Q Devil's advocate?
A I'd say he is Fairhope's devil advocate, not mine. I'm just an avenue.
Q So, it is your purpose to use the frog as Fairhope's devil's advocate?
A Not for me, he uses my hands and my ability to write because it's difficult for a frog to do so.
Q Well, you obviously put the words in the frog's mouth.
A No, the frog does.
Q Well, someone reduces it to paper.
A Yeah, I put it on the paper after he gives it to me. My dialogue with the frog is recorded and delivered to the paper.
Q Well, I don't want to be confused on this issue, but do you maintain this frog is a living, speaking being that you communicate with?
A Oh, sure, yes.

~

Buddy Brown regularly reviews medical records in preparing for his plaintiffs' cases. He recently sent me a portion of a medical record from an out-of-state hospital. The medical record reported a CT scan as having been done on the patient's skull, which revealed a medical finding of "subarachnoid hemorrhoid." Believe it or not, some citizens in that state accuse Alabamians of being backward.

~

David Hudgens shared the following story. One of David's former law partners repeatedly bragged about his wonderful legal secretary. After listening to this bragging, the senior partner of the law firm decided he was going to "steal" this legal secretary. Once the senior partner was able to persuade the legal secretary to work for him, he discovered that the secretary was completely incompetent. The senior partner was so embarrassed about having "stolen" the secretary that the secretary, despite poor job performance, stayed in his employ for twenty years.

Court Stories: Two Military Justice Stories

Our system of military justice also produces many amusing and unusual situations. The humanity of the actors often shines through, in spite of the more rigid decorum that exists in our military courts.

Lieutenant Commander Gus Lott, formerly of Bay Minette, witnessed a Captain's Mast (nonjudicial disciplinary hearing) on board a Navy ship at which the following exchange occurred.

The sailor who was on trial had a record which was replete with previous violations of the Code of Military Justice.

After the sailor was found guilty, the Captain told him all the possible sentences for the violation in question and then asked, "Is there anything you would like to say before the sentence is passed upon you?"

The sailor slowly took his wallet out of his pocket, opened it, held it up to his mouth like a radio and spoke the following words from the television series *Star Trek,* into the wallet, "Beam me up, Scotty!"

~

While he was on active duty with the Navy JAG Corps, one of attorney Larry Moorer's clients was a foreign national who worked for the Navy. The client had traded in a used car with an automatic transmission for what he thought was a new car identical to the one he had traded in. He stated that he wanted to sue the car dealership because they sold him a car "with too many gas pedals." Mr. Moorer had to explain the difference between a standard and automatic transmission to him.

3

Courthouse at Blakeley

History: County Seat at Blakeley

The seat of justice in Baldwin County moved from Dumfries to Blakeley and the following Act, which established Blakeley as the site of the County Courthouse, was passed on December 16, 1820:

> *SEC.* 4. AND BE IT FURTHER ENACTED, That the seat of justice or courthouse for the said county of Baldwin, as established by the first section of this act (which changed the boundaries of Baldwin County) be, and the same is hereby fixed in the town of Blakeley.
>
> *SEC.* 5. AND BE IT FURTHER ENACTED, That Cyrus Sibley, James W. Peters, Francis B. Stockton, and Benjamin

J. Randall, be and they are hereby appointed commissioners, a majority of whom shall have power and authority to procure by donation, or purchase at the expense of the county, a lot of ground in the said town of Blakeley, of such size as may in their opinion be suitable for the purpose of erecting thereon a courthouse and jail; and the said commissioners, or a majority of them, shall have power to contract with some person or persons for building the said court-house and jail as aforesaid, on such plan and in such manner as they may think proper; PROVIDED the sum for the said buildings shall not exceed the sum of two thousand dollars.

SEC. 6. AND BE IT FURTHER ENACTED, That the county court of the said county of Baldwin, be, and they are hereby authorized and required to lay such tax on the persons and property of the inhabitants of said county liable to taxation in other cases, as shall be sufficient to defray all the expenses to be incurred under this act: PROVIDED the tax so laid shall not exceed the sum of two thousand dollars.

SEC. 14. AND BE IT FURTHER ENACTED, That the court-house and jail at McIntosh's Bluff, in the county of Mobile, as established shall be sold by order of the county court of Mobile; and the moneys arising from said sales shall be equally divided between the counties herein named, to be applied to county purposes.

History: Blakeley's Trees of Justice

Some of the bricks from the Blakeley Courthouse mentioned in the foregoing Act are still at the site of the old courthouse, as well as some historic trees as mentioned in an article by Neil Letson that appeared in the October 22, 1981, edition of the *Mobile Register:*

> The Blakeley community grew rapidly to become an important center for boatyards, factories, and the good life.…Blakeley was designated the County Seat and the

first trials were held outdoors underneath the canopy of a large Live Oak, called the 'Jury Tree.' No one can say for sure how this tree was selected, but a person could speculate that its large shade producing canopy and the comfort provided the judge who sat on the main fork made this tree an ideal choice. The judge must have approved because he held sessions under the tree until a courthouse was built. To the defendant awaiting judgment, the 'Jury Tree' must have caused anxiety, but perhaps even more worrisome to the accused was the tree located just 100 yards away towards the Tensaw River called the 'Hanging Tree.' Another Live Oak, this Spanish Moss–laden tree gives no indication of its former use except for what some people claim are rope marks located midway along a huge horizontal limb about 15 feet above the ground. There are no estimates of how many times the 'Hanging Tree' was used, but it is certain the tree's services declined as did the town of Blakeley.[7]

Court Stories: Out of Our Mouths

Proverbs 25:11 says, "A word aptly spoken is like apples of gold in settings of silver," and I have particularly enjoyed some aptly spoken remarks of friends, some of whom are lawyers, through the years.

~

In discussing a particularly lazy local government official, J. B. Blackburn referred to him as "a barnacle on the ship of state."

~

When Judge Harry D'Olive, Sr., described a local candidate who had shocked everyone by winning an election, he told me, "that fellow being elected to public office is like a dog who chases

[7] Courtesy of the Mobile Register © 1981. All rights reserved. Reprinted with permission.

a police car and catches it. Now that he has got it, he won't have a clue what to do with it."

~

My father's expression for people who talk big but accomplish little was, "Big thunder, no rain."

~

When I offered to pay the tip after my colleague, Norborne Stone, treated me to a meal in a local restaurant, he remarked, "If I am going to get the piano, I'll get the stool too!"

~

Norborne's way of reminding me to get a haircut continues to be, "Sam, I am so sorry to learn of the untimely death of your barber."

~

Norborne facetiously told me he was thinking about leaving a last will and testament that simply reads: "Being of sound mind and disposing memory, I spent it all!"

~

Jim Reese's father gave him this advice when he went into business, "Jim, when you are sitting at your desk, one-half of the people you talk with will be smarter than you are, and the other half will not be smarter. Your problem is, you won't know which half is which."

~

One client shared this lamentation with me: "My son was a real jackass before I sent him off to college. When I got him home, I had an *educated* jackass on my hands!"

Court Stories: More Tales

During a law school examination at the University of Alabama Professor Gerald Gibbons saw a young man in the back of the classroom flipping a coin, slapping the coin on his wrist, checking the coin, picking up his pencil, and then writing on the examination paper.

Mr. Gibbons walked to the back of the classroom and said to the student: "I can't believe this. Your entire grade will be based on this one examination Are you deciding whether to write True or False on each question by flipping a coin?"

The student replied, "No, sir, I'm just checking my answers."

~

Frank Hollon, of Fairhope, contributed these stories.

Frank was appointed to represent a young man, D—, charged with selling crack cocaine. His alleged role in the "cocaine conspiracy" was that of a small-scale street dealer.

While meeting in the holding cell at the federal courthouse, Frank had the task of explaining the federal sentencing guidelines to his client. It went like this:

Hollon: D—, under the sentencing guidelines you have a mandatory sentence if you enter a guilty plea or if you're found guilty. In other words, you can't get probation even if the judge thinks you deserve it.

D—: How much jail time will I get?

Hollon: Well, under the guidelines, your minimum sentence will be 34 months. That's the shortest sentence the judge could give.

D—: Thirty-four months! That's almost a year. I can't serve no year.

After thinking a moment, Frank said, "Well, D—, it's gonna *seem* like more than a year."

~

Frank was retained recently to represent a man charged with driving under the influence of alcohol. During the meeting in his office he asked the routine question of whether or not the man had made the arresting officer angry. The man held up his right hand, which was missing half of the pinky finger. Frank asked the client what happened, and he suggested that he watch the police videotape.

On the videotape, the officer took the defendant through the routine roadside sobriety tests. The man repeatedly told the officer he was not intoxicated as he walked the line, stood up on one foot, and touched his nose. Finally, the officer asked the defendant to do the finger count. The officer explained to the man that he should start at his right index finger and count by touching each finger with his thumb in succession, "one, two, three, four" and then " four, three, two, one."

The man held his hand up very seriously and started to count—"one, two, three"—and then he yelled "three and a half" as he thrust his mutilated pinky finger toward the officer. The officer didn't think it was very funny and arrested the man immediately.

~

Jim Smith, who serves as municipal judge for Fairhope, contributed the following story:

> As we have seen in former tales, when alcohol is mixed with a trial, humorous things can happen.
>
> J—, a repeat offender, was back in Fairhope Municipal Court, again. He was frequently arrested for public intoxication, driving under the influence, or something similar. If out of jail on bail, he usually came to court intoxicated, and this evening was no exception. There was a question as to whether he could participate in the trial of his case. In order to resolve that situation, the city prosecutor, Tut Wynne, suggested, "Your Honor, I think we need to run an Intoxilyzer 5000 test to determine the percentage of *blood* in J—'s *alcohol system.*"

~

Charles Ham of Fairhope reminds us that a lawyer's first case in court can make the lawyer quite nervous. In his first case in Circuit Court, Charles stood in front of Judge Reid as the judge asked him a question regarding the case. Mr. Ham could not figure out how to best address the judge, and the only thing he could say was, "Yes, sir, Judge, Your Honor, yes, sir." Mr. Ham said he believed that at the moment he would have called the judge "Your Lordship" had he gone on.

~

One year when I was coaching little league baseball, I took a car full of players from Fairhope to Mobile for a game. As we were driving on Highway 98 through Daphne, we drove past the lot where construction was about to begin on our Daphne law office. I slowed the car down, proudly pointed to the lot, and proclaimed to the boys, "That's where my new office is going to be!" As soon as I made this proclamation, every boy in the car howled with laughter.

When I looked back at the lot, I realized there was a yellow portable toilet the construction crew had placed in the middle of the lot. Needless to say, the boys teased about my beautiful "law office" during the rest of the baseball season.

History: Attorney Qualifications

On Tuesday, March 23, 1819, the *Blakeley Sun* printed this note:

Requisite for Going Into Law

> A lady asked an old uncle, who had been an attorney, but had left off business, what were the requisites for going into law? to which he replied: "Why niece, it depends upon a good cause—secondly, a good counsel—thirdly, a good evidence—fourthly, a good jury—fifthly, a good judge—sixthly, a good purse—and, lastly, a good luck!"

The actual prerequisites for practicing law during the earlier years of the county were slightly different from those set out in the foregoing note in the *Blakeley Sun*. The following statutes set forth the actual prerequisites for the practice of law within Baldwin County as established by the legislature in 1807 and later in 1876:

1807

SEC. 1. BE IT ENACTED BY THE LEGISLATIVE COUNCIL AND HOUSE OF REPRESENTATIVES OF THE MISSISSIPPI TERRITORY IN GENERAL ASSEMBLY CONVENED, That no person shall hereafter be permitted to practice as counsel or attorney at law, in any of the courts of this territory, without previously producing to the County a license from the Governor (later the Court) of this territory, for the time being and in the presence of such court, shall take an oath to support the constitution of the United States; and also the following oath of office:— "I, A. B., do solemnly swear, (or affirm), that I will honestly demean myself in the practice as counsel or attorney: and will, in all respects, execute my office according to the best of my knowledge and abilities." And if any person shall presume to practice as counsel or attorney, without being licensed and qualified as aforesaid, he shall forfeit the sum of two hundred dollars for every case he shall prosecute or defend, in any court in this territory; one half to the use of the informer, the other half to the use of the territory; to be recovered by action of debt in any court of record: PROVIDED That nothing herein contained shall be so construed as to prevent or deprive any citizen from the privilege of personally prosecuting or defending any suit in which he may be a party.

SEC. 2. AND BE IT FURTHER ENACTED, That every person that hath already been, or shall hereafter be convicted of any felonious crime, shall be incapable of obtaining such licenses;...

SEC. 3. AND BE IT FURTHER ENACTED, That if the judges of the superior courts, from their own observation, detect any malpractice in the said courts, in any counsel or attorney of those courts; or if complaint in writing be made to them of such malpractice in the said courts, or in the county courts of any county the party accused shall be summoned to show cause why an information should not be filed against him: and if such information should be ordered, and the counsel or attorney so offending should be found guilty of the matter therein charged, the said judges of the superior courts may either suspend his license during a certain time, or vacate it altogether, as they shall judge most proper; first ordering a jury to be impaneled for the trial of such information. And the judges of the superior and justices of the county courts, shall have power to fine an attorney for misbehavior or contempt.

Requirements to Practice Law in 1876

Section 780—Code of Alabama of 1876

(861). WHO MAY PRACTICE AS ATTORNEYS. The following persons are only entitled to practice in the courts of this state:

1. Those who have been regularly licensed under the laws of this state, before the adoption of this Code.
2. Those who are hereafter admitted by a license from the supreme court, the court of chancery, or a circuit court.

(862). EXTENT OF LICENSE. Those who have been regularly licensed under the laws of this state, can practice only in such courts as their license authorizes them; those who are hereafter admitted to the supreme court, may practice in all the courts in this state; and those admitted by any chancery or circuit court may practice in any court of the state, except the supreme court.

(863). WHO MAY BE LICENSED. Any male of the age of twenty-one years, of good moral character, and who possesses the requisite qualifications of learning and ability, is entitled to admission to practice in any or all the courts of this state.

(864). APPLICATION FOR LICENSE. For the purposes of admission, he must apply to the supreme court, the court of chancery, or the circuit court, and must show:

1. That he is of the age of twenty-one years, which proof may be made by his own affidavit.

2. That he is of good moral character, which may be proved by certificate, or other evidence satisfactory to the court.

(865). EXAMINATION OF APPLICANT. The applicant must also be examined in open court, touching his knowledge:

1. Of the law or real property.
2. Of the law of personal property.
3. Of the law of pleading and evidence.
4. Of the commercial law.
5. Of the criminal law.
6. Of chancery and chancery pleading.
7. Of the statute laws of the state.

(867). MINORS MAY BE LICENSED. Circuit judges and chancellors may license minors, if possessing the maturity, character and attainments requisite, but the minors so licensed shall be precluded from pleading infancy in any civil proceeding against them.

(868). SUPREME COURT MAY APPOINT COMMITTEE. The supreme court may, at its discretion, appoint a committee of three members of its bar, to examine an applicant for license, either privately or in open court, and must grant or refuse license according to the report of such committee.

(869). OATH OF ATTORNEY. Every attorney, before commencing practice, must take an oath to support the constitution of this state, and of the United States, and not to violate the duties enjoined on him by law; which oath must be filed in the office of the clerk, or register of the court by which he is licensed.

Court Stories: More Tales

Attorney Norborne C. Stone, Jr., of Bay Minette defended a condemnation case filed by a power company. The power company filed the action in order to condemn a right-of-way across a local farmer's potato field. A power company representative had tried to persuade the farmer to give the power company the right-of-way across his field full of potatoes.

The power company representative asked, "Sir, why won't you give us the right-of-way over your field? Don't you think electricity is necessary?"

The farmer replied, "What kind of silly question is that? Don't you think potatoes are necessary?"

~

Joe Riddle of Bay Minette contributed this story about his grandfather, who was an engineer on a steam-run locomotive. His locomotive ran low on steam in a town with a courthouse near the railroad tracks. It was a very hot day and all the windows in the courthouse were open due to the heat. As the engineer was putting wood in the burner to generate steam, black smoke was pouring out of the engine's smokestack. The wind was blowing the black smoke directly in through the courthouse windows.

An irate judge came out of the courthouse and ordered the engineer to move the locomotive. The frustrated engineer replied, "I will comply with your order, Judge, as soon as I can generate enough steam!"

~

The following story involved the sleeping juror. Shortly after the testimony began on the first day of one of Judge Charles Partin's first civil jury trials, one of the jurors hearing the case fell asleep. Instead of waking up after a short catnap, the juror continued to sleep throughout much of the day's testimony.

Judge Partin knew the trial would last several days, so at the end of the first day's testimony, he carefully instructed the jury not to discuss the testimony they had heard with their families or friends. He then dismissed the jurors and they walked in a line past the bench on their way to the door. As the somnolent juror filed by the bench, he turned to Judge Partin and said, "You don't have to worry about me saying anything about the trial, Judge. I'm going home and telling my family I slept all day long."

~

One defense attorney stood up in front of the jury after a long-winded and boring first closing argument by the plaintiff's counsel and began his closing as follows:

"I'm surprised one of your jurors didn't just get up and leave during that long tirade! That closing reminded me of a story my preacher told me about a minister who, one Sunday, preached forty minutes on the Book of Hosea, forty minutes on Ezekiel, and forty minutes on Amos, then looked at the congregation and said, 'Now what place shall we give Obadiah?'

"One man in the back of the church stood up and said, 'He can have my place. I'm going home to dinner.'"

~

One old Baldwin County yarn is about a local loafer who came into the courthouse and angrily declared, "I have never been so mad in all my life. I had been standing in the same spot outside for hours just minding my own business when a man walked up and tied his horse to me!"

~

One old story told to me by John Chason involved the first Shakespeare production using local actors ever to be held in a small, rural Alabama town. After the actor playing Othello murdered Desdemona, he dramatically exclaimed, "Forsooth, what have I done?"

A drunk had wandered into the play late and did not really know what was going on. When he heard and saw this scene, he bolted to his feet and shouted, "I'll tell you what you've done, you maniac! You just killed the only lady of the night in this town!"

~

Harwell Coale contributed the following story about an experience he had while he was working with a large law firm. David Bagwell was a new lawyer with the law firm whose office was next to Harwell's. The law firm demanded long hours of each lawyer, and at 9:00 one night, Harwell heard a scream come out of David's office. He ran into David's office and found him pounding his fists on the table and moaning that his "whole life [was] over."

Harwell asked him what had happened, and David said, "Contrary to what they taught us in law school, I let the statute of limitations expire on a claim I should have filed." Harwell then asked David when the statute of limitations ran out on the claim, and David advised him the statute "ran today."

Harwell said, "We still have three hours; let's get the client's case filed." They prepared the complaint and took it to the circuit clerk's home shortly before midnight and filed it with the circuit clerk prior to the expiration of the statute. David learned a valuable lesson in perseverance, and his life was kept from being "over" during his first year in law practice.

History: Juries Past and Present

Although we still have experiences in court that are similar to those of our predecessors, the following grand jury list from the Fall Term of Circuit Court in 1866 made me realize the great differences in the constitution of our past and present juries. None of the jurors on this 1866 list were from today's larger county municipalities, and only four different occupations were listed.

Minutes of the Circuit Court of Baldwin County, State of Alabama, Commencing Fall Term AD 1866

State of Alabama *
Baldwin County *

I, C. W. Wilkins, Judge of the Probate Court, in and for said County and State, do hereby certify that on the twentieth day of September, AD 1866, the following named persons were drawn as Grand Jurors, for said County for the Fall Term of the Circuit Court of the County aforesaid, AD 1866, to-wit:

No.	Names	Residence	Occupation
1	Thaddeus C. Barlow	Mt. Pelier	Planter
2	Douglas W. Harris	Jack Spring	Planter
3	James D. Driesbach	Little River	Planter
4	John Killcreas	Stockton	Planter
5	Martin Lowell	Black Water	Planter
6	Ralph R. King	Tatemville	Manufactor of Tur.
7	Christopher Thompson	Blakeley	Mechanic
8	Frank J. McCoy	Hollywood	Manftr Turpentine
9	Price	Hollywood	Manufactor of Tur.
10	Francis B. Long	Blakeley	Planter
11	Aaron Taylor	Ridge Road	Planter
12	Murphy M. McMillan	Stockton	Mechanic
13	John P. Miles	Blakeley	Mechanic
14	Origen Sibley	Blakeley	Manftr Lumber
15	Uriah A. Barlow	Stockton	Mechanic
16	John Greenwood, Jr.	Greenwood	Manufter Turpentine
17	Thomas Loftis	Montrose	Mechanic
18	Hiram Taylor	Ridge Road	Mechanic

Given under my hand this 20th day of September, A D 1866.

Attest, C. W. Wilkins, Judge

History: The Relocation of Court from Blakeley to Daphne

Blakeley was established about twelve miles above Daphne on the Tensaw River by a group of enterprising citizens from the New England states. There were factories, hotels, cotton presses, stores, churches, a newspaper (*The Blakeley Sun*), and many beautiful homes. It was incorporated in 1815, and by 1828 it is believed to have had about four thousand inhabitants.

The town, however, did not survive long after 1828. After the scourges of yellow fever in 1826, and again in the 1830s, its population became scattered, and the remaining citizens moved to healthier locations.

Due to the plague, incoming shipping and traffic were closed off from the region, and by the early 1830s anyone who was still alive evacuated the city. The courthouse, presented quite a predicament, as it then stood empty and abandoned in the dead city. The court system was moved to Mobile, where it stayed for approximately 40 years. In 1868 a resolution passed by the Alabama Legislature placed the new courthouse in Daphne, where it would remain until 1901.[8]

[8]Nuzum, *History of Baldwin County,* pp. 69–76.

4

History: Some Early Twentieth Century Lawyers

Hawkins, Hall, Gilmer, Magney

William Henry Hawkins graduated in law from the University of Alabama in 1905. He began his law practice in Bay Minette in 1910, and continued until his death in September 1945. He was described affectionately as "a quiet gentleman" by one of his colleagues who knew him well.

Leslie Hall and Thomas Gilmer practiced law in Bay Minette for a number of years. Lloyd Magney was Foley's first attorney.

William Henry Hawkins

Leslie Hall

Thomas Gilmer

Lloyd Magney

Following are accounts of some of the attorneys who moved their practices from Daphne to Bay Minette when the county seat was moved in 1901.

Abner J. Smith

Abner J. Smith

Abner J. Smith played an important role in the history of Baldwin County. He was a lawyer in Kentucky and served as Commissioner of Schools in Jefferson County, Kentucky. He came to Baldwin County to do some title work for a client at the courthouse in Daphne. While he was here, he met Pearl Kessler, the lady who would later become his wife. He mailed the title work to his client and never moved back to Kentucky, opening a law office in Daphne to handle primarily civil cases. While he lived in Daphne, he bought *The Daphne Times* at a Sheriff's Sale for $75, changed the name to *The Baldwin Times,* and served as editor and publisher of the paper while continuing in law practice. The following are excerpts from an article entitled "The Story of the Baldwin Times," which was written by Gene Thomley and is reprinted with permission of *The Baldwin Times:*

> For the meager sum of $75, $15 down and $10 per month, Abner J. Smith assumed control of the paper in 1894, editing it longer than anyone else. The plant then consisted of a subscription list of 250, not half of them paid up, and Mrs. Smith, his widow, recalled having as many as 50 bushels of potatoes at a time, received in payment for subscriptions.
>
> The motto of the paper was "The Greatest Good to the Greatest Number." Throughout Mr. Smith's control as editor, he worked for the progress of the county and strove to improve its condition when the county barely contained 10,000 people.

> After the courthouse moved to Bay Minette in 1901, the paper moved with the county government and shortly thereafter...the first issue of the paper here was issued, with a special edition on the dedication of the courthouse. Mr. Smith continued to guide the destinies of the Times, but his health had been steadily failing and on January 12, 1905, he sold the paper to The Baldwin Times Publishing Company...
>
> His health improved somewhat, Abner Smith resumed ownership of the paper June 8, 1911, and continued until near his death in February, 1922. After his death, his widow, Mrs. Pearl Kessler Smith, sister of Jesse Kessler, clerk of the probate court, edited the paper in an admirable manner until July 6, 1922.

The editions of the *Baldwin Times* in the Archives in Montgomery indicate that on October 17, 1901, the newspaper was published in Daphne, Alabama. On October 24, 1901, the newspaper was first published in Bay Minette. Abner J. Smith became the first lawyer to practice in Bay Minette, moving both the newspaper and his law office from Daphne in October of 1901.

Stone, Hall, Jenkins

The classified advertisements for law firms during 1901 indicate that the lawyers in Daphne moved their practices to Bay Minette when the Court records were moved. According to these advertisements, Frank S. Stone was the second Bay Minette practitioner, having moved his law office to Bay Minette from Daphne on approximately December 5, 1901. Stone was certainly one of the most colorful characters in our local bar's history. He was born on June 12, 1863. The circuit court docket sheets reflect that his legal career began in Baldwin County on October 28, 1895, with an appearance in Court as Solicitor.

Frank S. Stone, Jr.

The third lawyer to move his practice from Daphne to Bay Minette was Oscar Hall, and the fourth lawyer to open a Bay Minette office was Sam C. Jenkins, who began his practice on approximately April 24, 1902.

Court Stories: "Mr. Frank"

"Mr. Frank" was famous for his sense of humor and his ability as a trial lawyer. His office was in the same building as a lawyer named Mr. Sam Jenkins. When Frank Stone left his office, he would put a sign on his door that read, "Gone Fishin'! If you need a lawyer you can go next door and see Sam Jenkins or you can go to H—. It's the same thing."

The Honorable Frank Stone aboard his favorite donkey

~

Frank Stone was one of the attorneys who assisted with the defense of Frank Boykin against criminal charges. Frank Boykin was acquitted of the charges, and after the case Frank Stone, who was known for spending every dime he made, drove back to Bay Minette in the "biggest finest car anyone in Bay Minette had ever seen." Frank Stone's wife received a dozen roses from Frank Boykin on her birthday every year for the rest of her life as a token of Mr. Boykin's gratitude.

~

One case Frank Stone defended involved the purported theft of a goat. Frank Stone's client was poor and Frank accepted one-half of the goat as his fee. During his closing argument, Frank Stone argued that his client "ain't got no more of that goat than I do."

~

One day Frank Stone left Daphne, bought a load of redfish at a fish store in Mobile, and brought them back home with him. He told everyone in town that he had caught the redfish by using liver as bait. People who lived in Daphne at the time said that the town stayed sold out of liver for weeks after the dissemination of Frank Stone's tall tale.

~

"Mr. Frank" was once defending a man charged with moonshining in a jury trial. He cross-examined the FBI agent who arrested his client and the FBI man in his testimony continued to use the colloquialism "stump hole water" to describe the bottled moonshine. Frank Stone asked him, "What did the bottled substance look like?" The FBI man answered "stump hole water." Mr. Frank asked, "What did it taste like?" The FBI man answered, "stump hole water." In his closing statement, Frank Stone argued to the jury that if the substance looked like stump hole water, and tasted like stump hole water, it must have actually been stump hole water rather than moonshine. This argument won an acquittal for his client.

~

Frank Stone looked for every advantage for his clients. He named his son after a local circuit judge, possibly to improve his chances in the judge's court.

~

A bet with Probate Judge Charles Hall on who would win the governor's race of 1914 earned Frank S. Stone a ride around the Baldwin County courthouse in the wheelbarrow shown on the next page. When Henderson won the election, Stone, then county solicitor for Baldwin County, was declared winner of the bet and is shown ready for his trek around Courthouse Square. Joseph B. Blackburn beat the drum for the occasion.

The boy with the black hat directly above Joseph Blackburn is his grandson, J. B. Blackburn, who practiced law in Baldwin County for over fifty years prior to his death.

An Election Where Push Came to Shove?

Frank Stone occasionally celebrated away from home after winning a case. Once he went and stayed at the Cawthorn Hotel in Mobile for a week-long party. His wife finally went to retrieve him, and after she came to the front desk, the manager called Mr. Frank's room and warned him that she was on the way up to his room.

When Mr. Frank heard the knock on the door, he said, "Who is it?"

His wife said, "Frank, this is Alice."

To which he replied, "Go away woman! I'm married to the sweetest woman in the world in Bay Minette, Alabama, and I don't allow any women around here!" This reply gained the forgiveness of Frank's wife.

~

Frank Stone also fancied himself as a cook and was particularly proud of the following recipe:

STONE'S FAMOUS BARBECUE SAUCE

Following proportions for medium size hog (preferably a RAZOR BACK SHOAT)

VINEGAR	*One Pint.*
BUTTER	*1 Pound.*
PAPRIKA	*2 Tablespoonsful.*
CURRY	*2 Tablespoonsful*
TABASCO	*1 Teaspoonful*
WORCHESTER SAUCE	*Half Pint bottle.*
TOMATO CATSUP	*One Pint bottle.*
GARLIC	*4 Pods mashed.*
ONIONS	*6 Medium sized ones chopped fine.*
LEMONS	*Juice of Six.*
MUSTARD POWDER	*Half Teacupful.*
SALT & PEPPER	*To suit taste.*

Melt butter, add onions and garlic, simmer slowly don't boil, stir in vinegar and lemon juice, add the other ingredients, paprika and curry last. Make mop of clean cheesecloth and baste carcass often, catching drippings, add to sauce. Cook shoat to golden brown.

AND THEN

WASH YOUR FACE**ASK THE BLESSING WITH DUE REVERENCE**GREASE YOUR MOUTH**DRAW NIGH** TAKE BIG MOUTHFULS**FILL UP TO REPLETION** SING A SONG IN LONG METER**REST FIVE MINUTES**

Smoke Corn Cob Pipe filled with cut plug***seek a cool sequestered spot, go to sleep and dream of sweet things. The above treatment will positively cure hunger, starvation, dyspepsia, corns, ingrowing toenails, baldness and inflammatory rheumatism.

IF NOT RELIEVED CONTINUE TREATMENT

The above Barbecue is best served WAY DOWN IN BALDWIN ON THE BANKS OF BON SECOUR AT FRANK STONE'S CAMP.

P.S. Vacant space after eating the above can be filled with Bon Secour plants and broiled trout.

THIS IS A GREAT LIFE IF YOU DON'T WEAKEN.

/s/ Frank S. Stone
Country Lawyer & First Class Cook.

History: One Interesting Baldwin Investor

One of the initial stockholders of Bay Minette Land Company was P. T. Sherman. He was the youngest son of the Civil War Union general, William Tecumseh Sherman. P. T. Sherman purchased his Bay Minette Land Company preferred stock on August 26, 1907.[9]

History: The "Stolen" Courthouse

The well known story of the "stealing of the courthouse" from Daphne by a group of Bay Minette citizens is reprinted below from *The Story of Daphne* with permission of author Mrs. Florence D. Scott.

> Prior to 1901, as a result of careful planning, Bay Minette decided that the governmental center for the County should be at Bay Minette and they had included a Court House Square when the town was laid out and actually built a Court House.
>
> An account of the Court House transfer appeared in the *Mobile Press Register* of Sunday, January 20, 1956, as told by Mr. E. J. Norris of Mobile, who was a member of the group from Bay Minette forty-five years before, as follows: "There had been talk of moving the Court House

[9]From original stockholder records of Bay Minette Land Company, used by permission of Ms. Elizabeth Duryea, President.

from Daphne to Bay Minette for some time before we actually got around to moving it. As I remember, J. D. Hand of the Hand Lumber Company at D'Olive was instigator of the plan to forcibly move the county seat to Bay Minette. I think there were fifteen or twenty of us in the group. We started out in the late afternoon from Bay Minette in wagons and buggies; some of us carrying shotguns and others pistols, but we never had any trouble. We arrived in Daphne around twilight and camped on the outskirts of the town until it was dark enough to cover our activities, then we moved down to the Court House.

"Advance plans had been made for the removal of the records and Hand and Sheriff George Bryant had arranged everything so all we had to do was walk into the Court House and walk out with the records and take them to Bay Minette. We had already erected a new Court House in Bay Minette and all that was necessary was to bring the records from Daphne and place them in the building."

The newspaper account goes on to say that, according to Mr. Norris, a prisoner in the jail helped pack the records into a wagon and was taken back to Bay Minette as the first prisoner in the new jail. With the help of convict laborers to do the heavy work, it took approximately five hours to sack the Court House records and several more hours to make the trip to Bay Minette in those days when roads were bad and travel was slow. Mr. Norris said further: "After we had moved the Court House, there was nothing else for the Judge to do but come down to Bay Minette and hold Court. Daphne made a few futile attempts to have the Court House moved back." (At the time of the transplanting, Mr. Norris was nineteen.)

The same paper also quotes from an article appearing in the old *Mobile News-Item* of October 13, 1901, which gives a slightly different version from that of Mr. Norris and [goes] into more detail inasmuch as it was written while the news was "hot." Information gleaned from the story declared that the State Legislature approved and gave citizens of Bay

Minette the right to move the Court House from Daphne to Bay Minette but made no provisions for the removal. So a group headed by John D. Hand, J. B. Blackburn, and O. E. McMillan moved in on Daphne, secured the records and prisoners and moved them to the new Court House in Bay Minette.

The *News-Item* story of 1901 said Hand was Chairman of the Building Committee of the new Court House and had warned Sheriff Bryant they were going to move the county seat to Bay Minette. That paper's version of the story said the group arrived in Daphne shortly before Sheriff Bryant stepped off an Eastern Shore bay boat with a court injunction staying the removal of the records and prisoners from the premises of the Daphne building. It further stated Hand called the Sheriff aside and with Blackburn as spokesman told the Baldwin Sheriff they were going to move the records. A ruse was used to get inside the building; Blackburn told the Sheriff they had a prisoner they wanted locked up and produced a teen-aged boy wanted for assault. The Sheriff took the prisoner and brought him into the jail and Hand and several of the group followed. Once inside, they refused to leave. After pleading, the Sheriff said he was going to lock them all inside. According to the newspaper version, Hand said he didn't want to be locked inside, and, when the door was opened wide enough for him to leave, two men with concealed wire-cutters squeezed in. The Sheriff locked the door and departed. The men with the wire-cutters went to work and it was only a matter of hours before the front door was opened and the cages containing the records were safely packed in a wagon and en route to Bay Minette.

The paper said that Probate Judge Charles Hall personally supervised the moving of his records and everything was removed from the Circuit Court room, including the judge's desk. The kidnapping of the county seat marked

a bitter fight in which several prominent B
citizens actively engaged in fisticuffs at variou

The background for the legal authority
county seat from Daphne is given in the follo
from old copies of the *Baldwin Times,* at th
lished in Daphne.

In the issue of December 13, 1900: "Bill been
introduced in both houses of the General Assembly (Legislature) providing for the removal of the County seat from Daphne to Bay Minette."

In the issue of January 24, 1901: "1,500 voters petitioned the Legislature to move the County seat to Bay Minette from Daphne, while 500 favored its retention."[10]

History: The "Stolen" Courthouse Revisited

The following paragraphs are excerpts from an article about the events involving the moving of the county seat from Daphne, written by Judge Charles C. Partin III for the *Baldwin County Historical Quarterly* and reprinted by permission.

Several Baldwin County history books discuss the 1901 removal of the county seat from Daphne to Bay Minette, Alabama. One author describes the transfer as the "stolen courthouse." A wall mural in the Bay Minette post office depicts a surreptitious nighttime moving of books and records. This article does not propose to support or refute the claim of a "stolen courthouse," but to examine the facts surrounding the event as disclosed by court records and other public documents.

Exact planning, the cooperation of some public officials, two acts of the Alabama legislature, a lawsuit, and a courthouse construction predated the physical transfer. Four years later, the Alabama Supreme Court,

[10] Florence D. Scott, *Daphne* (Mobile, AL: Jordan Publishing Co., 1965), pp. 54–57

(after three appeals and the passage of another legislative act) determined the legality of the removal in Bay Minette's favor.

The first named defendant in the lawsuit, James D. Hand, was the prime instigator, strategist, and tactician of the change of the seat of government. A timberman and sawmill operator, he moved from Jemmison, Alabama, to Baldwin County, settling in D'Olive, then he moved to a sawmill community not far from Bay Minette. During the last decade of the nineteenth century, Hand began to acquire various interest in a nine-thousand-acre tract known as the Dennis-Howe lands....

Central to Hand's development scheme was that Bay Minette become the county seat of Baldwin County. He commissioned a survey of a portion of the Dennis-Howe Tract and a town plat, complete with residential districts, parks, a school, and a business district surrounding Courthouse Square. Hand, no doubt, met with Baldwin's legislators, and with officials of the L&N Railroad during the fall of 1900, prior to the convening of the next session of the Alabama Legislature....

With the exception of State Senator Daniel Dillon Hall of Tensaw, all elected officials of Baldwin County in 1900 lived in or near Daphne. Nevertheless, Hand prevailed upon Representative George H. Hoyle of Daphne and Senator Hall to support legislation to change the county seat to Bay Minette....

During November of 1900, Hand sent canvassers to the populated areas of the county seeking signatures on a petition supporting removal legislation....Edward Quincy Norton, as chairman of the Citizen's Committee, circulated a counter petition resisting removal. Some citizens attested that they signed both petitions. Representative Hoyle claimed that the removalist petition contained 1,344 names; but if contested entries were deleted, 1,115 remained as opposed to the 886 on Norton's resistance....

Nonetheless, the Act was passed by the Alabama Legislature on February 5, 1901, "To provide for the removal of the county seat of Baldwin County, Alabama, from Daphne in said county, to Bay Minette in said county."

After a contractor was finally successfully appointed in F. M. Dobson, construction began on the new courthouse and jail in Bay Minette a few days after May 23, 1901.

> However, before F. M. Dobson dug the first foundation footing, Gus B. Stapleton and others filed a lawsuit against Hand, and the other Board of Commissioners, and the Court of County Commissioners seeking a permanent injunction against the removal of the county seat from Daphne and the construction of a courthouse in Bay Minette....
>
> While the judge studied the legal arguments, Hand set in motion the physical removal for the county seat to Bay Minette. He and his wife, Mattie Hand, accepted a deed conveying a large tract of land lying north of the railroad from Hand Lumber Company....
>
> On October 8, 1901, Judge Hall stopped recording instruments filed in his probate office in Daphne. No more documents would be recorded in the Daphne courthouse. Since the plaintiffs failed to seek any type of temporary injunction to prohibit the transfer pending the litigation's conclusion, Hand personally determined to carry out the legislative mandate to remove the county seat of Baldwin to Bay Minette. The new courthouse in Bay Minette was completed, leaving the physical location of the county's records, books, and other property in Daphne as the only remaining impediment to Hand's plan.
>
> Accordingly, on Thursday, October 10, 1901, Hand notified his men to prepare to travel to Daphne to load up the county records and property. At 7:00 P.M., thirteen double-team wagons and a contingent of Bay Minette men divided into well-provisioned military-style companies departed for Daphne. The march continued until 2:00 A.M.

> Friday, when the group struck camp four or five miles from Daphne to await dawn. With first light, the men moved to within one mile of the courthouse. An advance guard proceeded to the brick building and called for the larger group to join it. Hand led Company "C" to the jail located behind the courthouse.
>
> Company "C" held in its custody Frederick Richardson, a teenager accused of breaking into a Mr. Lee's house at Hurricane Bayou the day before. After his arrest, Richardson was probably brought before J. C. Day, a Justice of the Peace and employee of Hand Land Company. When Sheriff Byrne opened the Daphne jail door to receive Richardson as a prisoner, Hand and his band entered at once carrying hammers, chisels, hatchets, and axes. After the bewildered lawman unsuccessfully ordered the band to leave, he then locked the group in the jail which, in short order, the men began to disassemble.
>
> After the physical relocation of the county seat, all county offices were kept in Bay Minette, and all terms of court were conducted there....[11]

The pending case ultimately made its way to the Alabama Supreme Court, and at the conclusion of the litigation, the court held that the removal of the county seat from Daphne to Bay Minette had been lawful.

[11] Charles Partin, "The 1901 Removal of Baldwin County's Seat Revisited, *Historical & Genealogical Quarterly* 3, nos. 1–2, combined editions (1991) and 3, nos. 3–4, combined editions (1991), Bay Minette, Alabama.

Judge Hall, Frank Stone, and Others Out for a Ride

Court Stories: More Tales

According to the following *Baldwin Times* excerpt, in 1899, the Alabama legislature enacted a statute taxing bicycle riders. This tax confirms the old saying that "no man, woman, or child is safe while the Alabama legislature is in session."

Poor Bicycle Rider Was Taxed

A tax of 25 cents on bicycle riders was imposed by the last legislature and the law is now in effect.

It also provides that the Probate Judge shall have ten cents for issuing each license, thus making a cost of 35 cents to each rider. [From the *Times* of April 13, 1899]

~

One colorful local character was Lex Fulbright, who served as the justice of the peace for many years. I am informed that when Mr. Fulbright held court, he would have his wife prepare a pot of coffee for the occasion. In order to add dignity to the court, he would wear a shirt, but he rarely wore any shoes or socks during a session of his court.

~

Circuit judge Charles Partin contributed the following story about a trial in his courtroom: He was daydreaming on the bench when the defense lawyer objected to a question. Before hearing the grounds, Judge Partin inadvertently sustained the objection; he then turned to the defense lawyer and said, "Wait a minute, what are the grounds for your objection?"

The defense lawyer responded, "Your Honor, I don't know but I choose the grounds you've sustained on!"

~

Allan Chason shared a story about a young lawyer whose first case was the defense of a man charged with a serious crime. The defendant faced a long term of imprisonment if convicted.

In his closing argument to the jury the lawyer argued, "The only person in this courtroom more scared than the defendant is me. This is my first trial!"

~

Attorney Jim Yance contributed the next two stories:

> In the late seventies or early eighties, Greg Breedlove and I tried a wrongful death medical malpractice case for the death of a man who died in surgery. He left no wife or children and his nearest relative was a cousin who was our administratrix. The jury was made up of twelve citizens of Baldwin County and, as usual, consisted of mostly farmer/ landowners, business people, and comfortable retirees—not exactly a blue-ribbon plaintiff's jury. At the end of a week-long trial, the jury returned a verdict in our favor....This was a record medical malpractice verdict at the time in

Baldwin County. After the case was over, Greg and I were walking to my pickup truck (I always drive my pickup truck to court when I try a case in Baldwin County) when we ran into one of the jurors on our case. He was a well dressed fortyish-year-old salesman for a pharmaceutical company. He congratulated us on our handling of the case and said he had enjoyed his jury service. Since he had broken the ice, Greg and I took the opportunity to explore his thoughts about the case (hoping he would tell us how brilliant we were and how our innovative approach made the difference with him). He looked at us seriously and said, "When that lawyer for the doctor got through with his opening statement, and his cross-examination of your first witness, we all concluded that if we were that doctor and had him for a lawyer we would just plead guilty and throw ourselves on the mercy of the court". Greg and I could not help but laugh all the way home and still do when we recall that occasion.

~

Another amusing event occurred during the trial of a nursing home medical malpractice case that Bobo Cunningham and I tried in the early nineties. We were representing the widow of a deceased eighty-year-old nursing home patient who had received some very bad treatment in a Baldwin County nursing home. There was no serious settlement offer by the defendant, so we had the opportunity to try what we knew was going to be an interesting case and, depending on how it tried, had the potential to be explosive.

It was one of those cases where the longer it went, the better it got, and we were proving most of our case through the defendant's records and nursing personnel. One of these nurses we had on the stand began to crumble and "spill all." She acknowledged that patients were not cared for properly, were not changed properly when their clothing and linens were soiled, that some nurses...were physically mistreating patients. This nurse hurt the defendant nursing home so badly that one of the defense attorneys felt he had to impeach her in any way possible. One of the first ways he "impeached" her was to prove that she had been previously charged with patient abuse herself by the State Board of Nursing (something we could not get into evidence during our examination of her).

Needless to say, the case did not go well for the defendants and a policy limits offer was made while the jury was deliberating. Bobo and I declined the offer and shortly thereafter the jury knocked with a verdict. As the jury was entering the jury box, I heard the courtroom door open and looked around to see one of the attorneys for the excess carrier entering the courtroom. He had apparently been sent to attempt to engage us in further settlement negotiations, but before he could do so, the jury returned the largest plaintiff's verdict in the history of Baldwin County. It is often true that in life and the trial of lawsuits, timing is everything.

History: A Baldwin African-American Publication

The following is excerpted from a February 6, 1986, article in the *Mobile Register* by Jackie Byrd.[12]

> Bay Minette's history includes a chapter of little-known fact regarding the publication of *The American Banner.* Printed from September 1899 through February 1902, the journal was published and edited by Stephen J. Boykin.
>
> In addition to publishing his paper for several years, the father of eight children also founded Baldwin's first public school for black students.

[12] Courtesy of the Mobile Register © 1986. All rights reserved. Reprinted with permission.

Jacqueline Cox, granddaughter of Stephen J. Boykin, and her husband, John Cox, who was one of the best court bailiffs in Baldwin County history.

The *American Banner* was printed in Bay Minette twice monthly and was apparently widely circulated. Subscription rates published in one edition gave costs of $1 for one year, 50 cents for six months, and 30 cents for three months. Boykin stressed that subscription payments were requested "strictly in advance."

Advertising solicitations were also part of the operation of the American Banner Publishing Company, which was situated in Boykin's home. Display-type notices cost advertisers $1.50 "per inch per month," while line ads were sold for 15 cents per line for one month.

Boykin's paper seemed to provide a number of services to the community. In addition to local, national and even international news, the *Banner* listed Louisville and Nashville train schedules for north- and southbound travelers, and gave farm and garden advice.

While the publication dispensed general news, Boykin directed much of his newsprint to black readers. The race-oriented paper included such columns as "Race Gleanings" and "Race Notes." Boykin urged his black readers to represent their race well so that others would take notice of black accomplishments.

The self-educated editor-teacher-school principal also used his publication to seek support for the founding of a "normal school" in Bay Minette in 1899....

The late editor is survived by one son, Alvin E. Boykin, 72, of South Section Street in Fairhope....

The elder Boykin would occasionally talk about the defunct newspaper, Alvin Boykin said, while a family collection includes ledgers and other records relating to the newspaper business.

"I am proud" of the newspaper produced by his father, Alvin Boykin said recently from the home he shares with his wife, Ida. Boykin noted that he has read a few editions of the old paper and they "seemed to have been very well done."

Like his father, Alvin Boykin was an educator, earning a master's degree in education. Alvin Boykin served for 25 years as principal of Anna T. Jeans School in Fairhope.

Stephen J. Boykin died in 1927, records show, but continued always to think like a newspaper man. According to his son, Boykin "always kept a ledger of everything that happened including the date, weather, and current events."

Advertisements from the Saturday, March 2, 1901, *American Banner* included the following:

****

C. J. CAMPBELL, Bay Minette, Ala., Magnetic and Mental Scientist, Cures all Diseases Without Medicine or Surgery. A graduate, with Diplomas and Degrees of four noted colleges of America in the science of curing disease without medicine. For thirty years a deep and intense student of Truth, a practical and scientific investigator. Large and increasing practice. Successful with the most complicated disease the best physicians have failed to cure enables me to offer the best service in healing and restoring the mind and body.

****

LESLIE HALL, Lawyer, Brewton, Ala. Practices in all Courts, State and Federal. Prompt Attention to all legal business.

****

FRANK STONE, JR., Attorney-at-Law, Daphne, Ala. Will practice in all the courts of Baldwin, Washington and Mobile counties.

****

History: An Earlier State Bar Convention

On July 2, 1925, the Alabama State Bar Association held its annual convention at the Colonial Inn in Fairhope. The menu from the convention was contributed by Wes Overton and states in part, "Doth not the appetite alter? A man loves the meat in his youth, that he cannot endure in his age."

Colonial Inn

5

History: Circuit Riding Judges and Their Stories

Prior to the formation of the Twenty-Eighth Judicial Circuit in 1948, the judges were "circuit riders" who came to the county seat for one-week terms of court several times a year. The photographs below are of circuit-riding judges from other counties who tried cases in Baldwin County during their terms on the Bench.

W. E. Clark, 1882
(Mobile)

John R. Thompkins, 1887
(Mobile)

William S. Anderson, 1896 (Mobile)

Samuel B. Brown, 1904 (Mobile)

Arthur E. Gamble

Arthur E. Gamble

Another judge who rode a circuit that included Baldwin County was Arthur E. Gamble. He was born in Greenville, Alabama, attended school in Greenville and graduated from the Marion Military and Collegiate Institute.

He passed his bar examination and was admitted to the bar on September 22, 1896. Judge Gamble began serving as the circuit judge for Baldwin County in 1911.

When Judge Gamble came to Bay Minette for a term of court, there were few nice hotel rooms in Bay Minette, so he would stay in a room at the home of Mr. and Mrs. W. C. Beebe. Mrs. Beebe mentioned to me that she remembered having to clean cigarette burns from the mantle on which Judge Gamble would inadvertently leave a lighted cigarette while studying pleadings in a case he was preparing to try.

Judge Gamble was well known for his personality and sense of humor. An incident illustrating his sense of humor occurred during one term of court when Judge Gamble was in Bay Minette trying cases. Attorney Elliott Rickarby, Sr., was trying a case against a local attorney who was known to imbibe too freely and was not sober when he appeared in court for this particular case. During the trial of the case, the inebriated lawyer got so mad at Elliott Rickarby that he swung at him and hit him with his fist. When this occurred, Judge Gamble recessed the trial and told the lawyer he would not allow him to apologize to the Court that day due to his inebriated condition but that he would allow him to do so the next day.

The next day when Court opened all the members of the local bar were there, including the offending lawyer. However, the lawyer was again not in a sober state. When Judge Gamble saw the members of the bar in court, he said, "I see a lawyer is here this morning who would like to apologize to this court."

The nervous offending lawyer stood up and, being confused due to his nervous condition, used the word "contempt" rather than the word "respect" in stating, "Your Honor, I would like to apologize to this Court. As you know, I have the utmost contempt for this Court."

A silence fell over the courtroom when the lawyer made this statement. Judge Gamble smiled benignly, looked down from the bench, and said in a wry tone, "I see you have."

John David Leigh

John David Leigh of Brewton, Alabama, succeeded Judge Gamble as judge of the circuit. He was born in Pollard, Alabama, on June 25, 1872, and died in Brewton, Alabama, August 23, 1936. His father was Norvelle Leigh, Sr., Probate Judge of Escambia County for twenty-four years. John David Leigh graduated from the University of Alabama with a law degree in 1894. He and his brother Norvelle Leigh, Jr., a former probate and circuit judge for Mobile County, went into practice together until Norvelle Leigh moved to Mobile. In 1919 Governor Kilby appointed John David

Leigh, Judge of the Twenty-First Judicial Circuit, which included Escambia, Baldwin, Monroe, and Conecuh Counties. In 1929, Judge Leigh went back into private practice until his death in 1936.

John David Leigh

Norvelle Leigh, Jr.

John Leigh's brother, Norvelle Leigh, Jr., is a good example of a "circuit-riding lawyer," having appeared in the Circuit Court of Baldwin County during the Fall 1898 Docket. According to his daughter, Mr. Leigh believed that "politics was everyone's business." Because of this belief, Mr. Leigh served as a delegate to the 1932 National Democratic Convention as a staunch Franklin D. Roosevelt supporter. Mr. Leigh even had a photograph signed by President Roosevelt that he kept in his living room. When Mr. Leigh determined that President Roosevelt "went against the Constitution by padding the Supreme Court," Mr. Leigh got so mad he placed the autographed Roosevelt photograph in the attic of his home facing the wall. There it remained until after Mr. Leigh's death many years later.

Francis William Hare

Francis William Hare was elected as a circuit judge in 1928 for the Twenty-First Judicial Circuit (then comprising Monroe, Conecuh, Escambia, and Baldwin Counties—Baldwin County was made a separate circuit in 1948) and served until his death on April 18, 1952. He was a resident of Monroeville, Alabama.

Judge Hare was born April 11, 1878, in Oak Bowery, Chambers County, Alabama. His brother and sister-in-law died at an early age, leaving three sons who were reared by Judge Hare along with his own children.

Shortly after graduating from Auburn, he joined the Alabama Volunteer Infantry and served in the Spanish-American War. He

Francis William Hare

entered the law school at the University of Alabama and graduated in 1901. He moved to Monroeville in September 1901 and enjoyed an active law practice there until he was elected circuit judge in 1928. During his law career, he also maintained offices in Evergreen, Brewton, and Bay Minette. As a judge, Francis Hare became widely known for his faculty of getting to the point of the case and simplifying the controversy.

Judge Hare was dignified and controlling on the bench. Attorneys Charles Hybart and John Chason were trying a case once, and Judge Hare fined Mr. Hybart $10 for repeating a question after having sustained an objection to the question. He made Mr. Hybart's law partner, John Chason, pay this fine. When court recessed, Judge Hare tried to remit payment of the fine to Mr. Hybart. Mr. Hybart was so upset he would not accept the money back.

Judge Hare used to stop at the home of Charlie Earle in Blacksher on his way home to Monroeville after a week of court in Bay Minette. "Mr. Charlie" would always give "the Judge" a drink of whiskey when he stopped in. One day Judge Hare stopped by and Charlie Earle wasn't in. Charlie's son, Jimmy Earle, who was an infant at the time, was the only one home. When the Judge knocked on the door, little Jimmy told Judge Hare, "I can show you where it is, but I can't reach the bottle, Judge!"

Once Judge Hare appointed a lawyer just out of law school to represent a defendant in a murder case. The young lawyer protested, "Your Honor, I am too inexperienced to represent this man. I don't know how to handle this case."

Judge Hare said, "Ed, just talk to the man and try to handle it."

The young lawyer again protested, "Judge, I just don't think that I am capable of handling this case."

Judge Hare said, "Ed, just go back there and tell him to do what you would do if you were in his shoes."

The young lawyer took his client out of the courtroom. About an hour later, Judge Hare started wondering where they had gone. After another hour, Judge Hare sent the bailiff to find the lawyer. The bailiff brought him back without his client. Judge Hare said, "Ed, where have you been and where is your client?"

The lawyer said, "I did what you said, judge, and told him what I would do under the same circumstances. About now he should be a good five miles away from here. He jumped out the window and started running as fast as he could away from this courthouse."

History: Other Lawyers and Their Stories

William Craig Beebe

William Craig Beebe

William Craig Beebe was born in Silver City, Mississippi, on November 1, 1890. He received his law degree from the University of Alabama in 1915. He was elected to the Alabama Legislature and served from 1927 through 1935. He was the attorney for the Governing Board of Baldwin County, the Town of Robertsdale, and the Town of Fairhope. He also served as the chairman of the Democratic Executive Committee. He served a second period in the Legislature from 1939 through 1943.

Mr. Beebe and Elliott Rickarby, Sr., practiced together in Bay Minette. During this time, Mr. Rickarby rode the train from Mobile to Bay Minette in order to practice in Baldwin County.

One story concerning Bill Beebe involved a trial between Mr. Beebe and Tolbert Brantley that took place shortly after Mr. Brantley had graduated from law school. The case was an ejectment action and Mr. Brantley was too inexperienced to know the law of ejectment well at the time. Mr. Beebe and Mr. Brantley were arguing the law to Judge Hubert Hall, and Mr. Beebe opened a *Southern Reporter* and started reading a case that was very favorable to his position. He read on and on, and the case sounded as if it were dispositive of the case at bar.

As he read, Mr. Brantley got more discouraged and thought to himself, "How in the world could he have found such a perfect case to support his argument?"

Finally, Judge Hall stopped Mr. Beebe in the middle of a sentence and said, "Bill, are you reading us the law, or are you reading Beebe?"

Mr. Beebe hung his head sheepishly and said, "Judge, I am reading Beebe".

One of Mr. Beebe's favorite stories involved a trip he made through a rural area of Baldwin County while running for public office. There was a politician there who was "stump speaking" and stated, "I grew up here, my parents grew up here, in fact, I was born and raised between two rows of corn in a field here." A heckler from the audience stood up and said, "By golly, the fellow is a pumpkin!"

Elliott G. Rickarby, Sr.

Elliott Garrow Rickarby, Sr., was born in September 23, 1873, in Mobile and died on March 27, 1952, in Fairhope. He attended Barton Academy and the University of Virginia. His daughter told me of the many times her father accepted a chicken or bushel of vegetables as a fee when his client was too poor to pay him.

Elliott G. Rickarby, Sr.

Henry D. Moorer

Henry D. Moorer was a successful lawyer who practiced in Bay Minette for a number of years during this period. He was born in 1889 and died in 1935.

Henry D. Moorer

Charles Hybart

Charles Hybart

Charles Hybart was from Hybart, in Monroe County, Alabama. He practiced in both Monroeville and Bay Minette. When his father died, he inherited the family store, which was a successful concern. According to his daughter, Mr. Hybart was a poor businessman with grandiose ideas. He bought oriental rugs in New York for the family store and tried unsuccessfully to sell these types of items in Hybart, Alabama. He went back to school and graduated in law from the University of Alabama in 1897. Mr. Hybart later became a fine criminal lawyer.

"Mr. Charlie" often thought a continuance would help in a criminal case. In one instance, his client was denied a continuance by a local judge despite Mr. Hybart's assertion that his client's health prevented a trial. Mr. Hybart had an ambulance bring his client to the courthouse and had him wheeled in on an operating table by two nurses. After the jury venire saw this display, the judge had no alternative but to grant the continuance.

In another case, he was employed to represent a wealthy man who was obtaining a divorce from his wife. The wife was so poor that without financial assistance from her husband she could not afford an attorney. Charlie Hybart's wife felt sorry for this woman and showed up on the day of the trial with the impoverished wife and Mr. Harry Seals, a renowned divorce attorney from Mobile, whom Mrs. Hybart had hired and paid out of her pocket to represent the woman in the proceeding.

Norborne Clarke Stone, Sr.

Norborne C. Stone, Sr.

Norborne Clarke Stone, Sr., was born July 15, 1887, in Bay Minette, Alabama, and graduated from the University of Alabama School of Law in 1917. He began his law practice with his father, Frank S. Stone, in the firm of Stone & Stone. He died at the age of thirty-three. One of his colleagues remembered him as, "the best young lawyer in Bay Minette when I started my practice." Another colleague told me "there are good book lawyers and good maneuverers. Norborne was a good maneuverer. A good maneuverer can see the stump in the road from a little farther away than the next fellow." This colleague went on to say, "I remember one time I surprised Norborne by catching him with a big plug of tobacco in his mouth at his office, and he said, "Boy, I'm glad it's you. Normally, every time I get a good chew in this office, some darn woman walks in."

Ralph Lee Jones

Ralph Lee Jones from Monroeville graduated from the University of Alabama School of Law in 1919. He received $300 per month to serve as solicitor for four counties, including Baldwin. He represented Baldwin County for a portion of his twelve years in the state legislature.

During his term as a legislator, the Baldwin County license inspector prepared a bill which passed in both the Senate and the House requiring any truck doing business in Baldwin County to have a license. At this time, a number of migrant field workers came to Baldwin County with trucks to gather potatoes for a period of six weeks. These migrant workers could neither afford nor qualify for the license required by the bill. If the bill was signed into law by the governor, the result would have been that a number of potato growers would have lost their potato crops due to not having help from the migrant workers. Sheriff Ramsey Stuart and Mr. Jones had the Baldwin County potato growers flood the governor with telegrams in opposition to the legislation. After several days of the telegrams, the governor called Mr. Jones and said, "If you'll call off the telegrams, I'll kill that bill!"

Ralph Lee Jones

Archie H. Elliott

Another past circuit solicitor was Archie H. Elliott, who served Baldwin County from August 1945 until the creation of the Twenty-Eighth Judicial Circuit in 1948. One memorable Baldwin County case that he tried involved a man who shot his wife and put her in the trunk of his car. The man was caught when some people at a gas station heard his wife moaning from the trunk of the car.

Archie H. Elliott

Court Stories: Laughs from Around the State

The following stories were contributed by my friend, Norman Jetmundsen, who practices law in Birmingham. Some are actual transcripts of court cases as reported on the internet.[13]

THE COURT: Next witness.
MS. OLSCHNER: Your Honor, at this time, I would like to swat Mr. Buck in the head with his client's deposition.
THE COURT: You mean read it?
MS. OLSCHNER: No, sir, I mean swat him in the head with it. Pursuant to Rule 32, I may use this deposition for any purposes, and that is the purpose for which I want to use it.
THE COURT: Well, it does say that (*pause*). There being no objection, you may proceed.
MS. OLSCHNER: Thank you, Judge Hanes.

(Whereupon Ms. Olschner swatted Mr. Buck in the head with a deposition.)

MR. BUCK: But, Judge—
THE COURT: Next witness.
MR. BUCK: We object.
THE COURT: Sustained. Next witness.

~

Q What is your brother-in-law's name?
A Borofkin.
Q What's his first name?
A I can't remember.
Q He's been your brother-in-law for years, and you can't remember his first name?

[13]Norman Jetmundsen, *Alabama Defense Lawyers Association Journal,* 16, No. 2 (October 2000), Montgomery, Alabama.

A No. I tell you I'm too excited. (*Rising from the witness chair and pointing to Mr. Borofkin.*) Nathan, for God's sake, tell them your first name!

~

Q Did you ever stay all night with this man in New York?
A I refuse to answer that question.
Q Did you ever stay all night with this man in Chicago?
A I refuse to answer that question.
Q Did you ever stay all night with this man in Miami?
A No.

~

Q Now Mrs. Johnson, how was your first marriage terminated?
A By death.
Q And by whose death was it terminated?

~

Q Ms. –, were you cited in the accident?
A Yes Sir, I was so 'cited I peed all over myself.

~

Q Doctor, did you say he was shot in the woods?
A No, I said he was shot in the lumbar region.

~

Q What is your name?
A Ernestine McDowell
Q And what is your marital status?
A Fair.

~

Q Are you married?
A No, I'm divorced.
Q And what did your husband do before you divorced him?
A A lot of things I didn't know about.

~

Q And who is this person you are speaking of?
A My ex-widow said it.

~

Q Do you know how far pregnant you are right now?
A I will be three months November 8.
Q Apparently the date of conception was August 8?
A Yes.
Q What were you and your husband doing at that time?

~

Q Mrs. Smith, do you believe that you are emotionally unstable?
A I should be.
Q How many times have you committed suicide?
A Four times.

~

Q Doctor, how many autopsies have you performed on dead people?
A All my autopsies have been performed on dead people.

~

Q Were you acquainted with the defendant?
A Yes, sir.
Q Before or after he died?

~

Q What happened then?
A He told me, he says, "I have to kill you because you can identify me."
Q Did he kill you?
A No.

~

Q Mrs. Jones, is your appearance this morning pursuant to a deposition notice which I sent to your attorney?

A No. This is how I dress when I go to work.

~

THE COURT: Now as we begin, I must ask you to banish all present information from your minds, if you have any.

~

Q Did he pick the dog up by the ears?
A No.
Q What was he doing with the dog's ears?
A Picking them up in the air.
Q Where was the dog at this time?
A Attached to the ears.

~

Q When he went, had you gone and had she, if she wanted to and were able, for the time being excluding all the restraints on her not to go, gone also, would he have brought you, meaning you and she, with him to the station?
MR. BROOKS: Objection. That question should be taken out and shot.

Court Stories: More Tales

An old lawyer representing a railroad company had a case against a very young lawyer. The case involved some cattle that were allegedly killed by a locomotive, and the young lawyer represented the owner of the cattle. The lawyers settled the case, and after the settlement, the old railroad lawyer decided he would teach his young colleague a lesson. "Son, there is one thing I would like to tell you now that this case has been concluded. Those cattle were worth a great deal, and you settled the case for too little money."

The young lawyer replied, "Now that you mention it, there is one thing I'd like to tell you. Those cattle wandered home from that railroad crossing yesterday."

~

In another case, a lawyer laboriously prepared a fifty-page brief in support of his position. He proudly put the brief before the local judge. Without opening the brief, the judge picked it up, felt its weight, looked up at the lawyer and said, "I'm ruling against you on this point."

The appalled lawyer gasped, "Why, Judge! You didn't even read my brief!"

The judge calmly replied, "If it took that many pages to say it, it must be a lie."

~

Shawn Alves, a young lawyer with our firm, was duly initiated into the legal profession when he took his first deposition.

During the deposition, an older lawyer took the cup of water that Shawn had brought along with him, dumped the water out, and proceeded to use it as a spittoon.

Later in the deposition, this lawyer whispered to Shawn, "I've been wearing these pants all week long."

As the deposition continued, another lawyer and the deponent threatened to "kick each other's a**."

Finally, when the court reporter was gathering the exhibits to include with the transcript, she discovered that one of the lawyers had mistakenly taken an original exhibit home with him.

~

Mary Murchison contributed the following story about her great-grandfather, George Marks. Mr. Marks was a Montgomery lawyer whose first case involved the defense of a man charged with stealing a turkey. The defendant was acquitted by a jury. Coincidentally, after the trial, the defendant tried to pay Mr. Marks his fee in turkey meat. The other lawyers in the Montgomery Bar were so amused when they heard the story that they gobbled like a turkey at Mr. Marks whenever they saw him. Mr. Marks was so rattled by their behavior that he never took another criminal case but rather limited his practice to legal problems involving real estate.

~

The following story was contributed by Floyd Enfinger:

During the early period of my private practice, I handled a substantial number of criminal matters and prided myself on being a good criminal attorney. Attorneys Mary Murchison and Margaret Thomas had been appointed to represent a defendant charged with several counts of burglary and who called himself "the Fox." The Fox professed his innocence, in spite of the fact that numerous items taken in the burglaries were discovered in his hotel room and in his coat pockets. His assertion of innocence was backed up only by an alibi that he was too drunk to recall any events on the night in question.

Margaret and Mary asked my advice as to how to best try this case, given the Fox's past criminal history and his alibi. They told me that the D.A. had offered an extremely favorable plea bargain involving a short jail term, and I quickly advised them to take this offer, as they had no chance to win the case. With his prior record and the number of cases involved, we all knew the Fox would probably be sent away for twenty or thirty years if he didn't plead guilty before trial.

When Margaret and Mary told me that the Fox wouldn't accept the plea bargain, I couldn't believe it. I told them I had no doubt I could persuade the Fox to accept, and thus solve their problem for them. I went to the jail with Margaret and Mary and met the Fox. He was about 6'6" tall, well built, and he towered over me.

I looked up and spoke to the Fox quietly at first and then in a stern manner and finally in a heated fashion before the Fox turned to Mary and said, "Who is this guy? Is he supposed to be a lawyer?" That remark was enough to send me into a rage and I told him in no uncertain terms what would happen to him if he went to trial. I berated him, verbally abused him, and questioned his judgment and intelligence. The only response I got from the Fox was, "I ain't doin' no time." I was so sure that I could accomplish what Margaret and Mary couldn't do, I tried even harder out of a sense of pride, but to no avail.

Prior to trial, the D.A. discovered that the police had returned the stolen goods to the owners, other evidence was lost, and no witnesses could be found. When the case was called for trial, the State had no choice but to dismiss the cases, and the Fox walked free. He smiled at me, reminded me of our confrontation in the jail, and laughed, "I ain't doin' no time."

~

Thomas B. Norton, Jr. contributed the following story:

While I was the Assistant District Attorney, I handled a number of juvenile court cases. After each case, I lectured the juvenile involved in an attempt to prevent future problems. After one such lecture, Judge Phyllis Nesbit, the Juvenile Court Judge, called me to the Bench and said, "Tom, you must have been a real hellion when you were young. You know precisely why these children did what they did, what they were thinking and what excuses they are going to give for their behavior."

~

Judge Nesbit herself contributed the following stories:

While Judge Nesbit was in private practice, a woman came to see her about her "wills." The woman had eight children and eight different wills. She told Judge Nesbit that a justice of the peace had prepared the wills in accordance with his incorrect advice to her that "she needed a different will for each child."

~

A number of years ago, a young man and woman were arrested for an offense in Daphne. The woman had a pet white mouse who stayed on her shoulder. Judge Nesbit signed an order to board the mouse at the veterinarian's while the woman was in jail. The vet put the mouse in a shoebox until the woman was released, and Judge Nesbit included the expense of boarding the mouse as part of the court costs to be paid by the young woman.

~

Louis Braswell shared the following story about a wise client who left in the middle of an important business meeting to attend his exercise class.

Louis Braswell said, "Abe, you are *indispensable* to this business. How can you leave this meeting?"

The wise client replied, "Louie, I drove by Pine Crest Cemetery this morning and thought about all my friends there who thought they were 'indispensable' to their businesses."

6

History: Baldwin County's Judges of Probate

Early Years

The following pages contain photographs of some of the individuals who served as probate judges for Baldwin County prior to creation of the Twenty-Eighth Judicial Circuit in 1948. During these years, the probate judge was an integral part of the local court system and an important local leader.

Judge Charles Hall's Probate Courtroom

Duties

Under Alabama law, the probate judge has always had diverse duties. The current law provides that the probate judge can approve an adoption, change a name, order condemnation of property, conduct a wedding, commit someone to a mental hospital, issue hunting, fishing, driving or business licenses and "decide who gets Aunt Hattie's blue vase."

History: Some of Our Probate Judges

Patrick Byrne	1827-1856
G. W. Wilkins	1856-1866
Osmyn P. Hall	1869-1870
William H. Gasque	1871-1892
Charles Hall	1893-1904
J. H. H. Smith	1904-1916
James M. Voltz	1917–1923
G. L. Lambert	1923–1924
William D. Stapleton	1924–1926
G. W. Humphries	1926–1935
G. W. Robertson	1935–1944

Patrick Byrne

William H. Gasque

Charles Hall

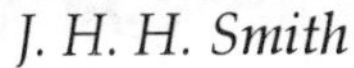

J. H. H. Smith *James M. Voltz* *G. L. Lambert*

William Stapleton *G. W. Humphries* *G. W. Robertson*

Court Stories: Probate Judges

The following story was told to me by Wilson Hall, a descendant of Judge Charles Hall. Major General E. R. S. Canby of the Union Army was the occupation general in Baldwin County at the close of the Civil War. The Union troops had burned the Hall home while Charles Hall was still a young boy. After losing everything, Charles Hall's father asked General Canby for food to feed his family until he could rebuild. General Canby kindly assisted the Halls during rebuilding. When Charles Hall grew up, he wished to thank the Union general for this kindness. General Canby died before Charles Hall met him. Judge Hall searched until he was able to find the burial place, then arranged through a minister in Indianapolis, Indiana, to place flowers on General Canby's grave as a token of his gratitude.

~

Judge W. R. Stuart served as both probate judge and sheriff of Baldwin County. During a woodland search for an escaped convict, Sheriff Stuart was attacked by the convict. Sheriff Stuart raised his pistol, aimed for the man's body and pulled the trigger. The bullet struck the man in his foot. After the arrest, the local citizens marveled at Sheriff Stuart's marksmanship. Several years after the incident, he confessed he was, in fact, *not* aiming at the convict's foot.

Courthouse at Daphne, Alabama
1868-1901

One family produced three of the County's earliest probate judges: Patrick Byrne (1796–1881), Peter Cornelius Byrne (1810–1878), and David Crawford Byrne all served as early Probate Judges of Baldwin County.[14]

[14]Regina Moreno Kirchoff Mandrell, *Our Family: Facts and Fancies* (Pensacola, FL: Perdido Press, 1988), pp. 539, 542.

7

History: Some Attorneys of the New 28th Circuit and Their Stories

Title 13(112(5), *Code of Alabama:* "At a general election in 1948, a judge and solicitor for the said 28th Judicial Circuit shall be elected....[On] the 1st Monday after the 2nd Tuesday in January, 1949....Baldwin County shall be and is hereby detached from the twenty-first judicial circuit and shall thereafter constitute and be the twenty-eighth judicial circuit of the State of Alabama."

Hubert Hall

Hubert Hall

Hubert Hall served as circuit judge from 1953 to1964, and practiced law for many years in Bay Minette. Judge Hall handled a case as an attorney in which his client was charged with negligently running off the road in his automobile and killing an expensive horse. Mr. Hall tried to convince the jury that the horse had been depressed and skittish and decided to commit suicide by jumping out in front of his client's car.

~

Ralph G. Holberg, Jr., of Mobile, was involved in a real property case before Judge Hall. In the case, Mr. Holberg's opposing counsel objected to a particular surveyor performing a court-appointed survey. In ruling on the objection, Judge Hall stated, "I know this land and I am convinced that a one-eyed baboon with a piece of string could provide the survey. Objection overruled."[15]

J. B. Blackburn

J. B. Blackburn

J. B. Blackburn was born in Bay Minette, Alabama, on September 21, 1900. He initially began to study law in 1919 but came back to Bay Minette in 1920. He drove a taxi cab and had other jobs in Bay Minette until the summer of 1926 when an experience serving on the jury convinced him he should practice law. He graduated from the University of Alabama School of Law in 1928 and began practice in Bay Minette. He also served as Baldwin County's first member of the Board of Bar Commissioners. He was recognized by his colleagues as an excellent student of the law.

J. B. was involved as a party in a case in which he was being represented by his son, Dan. I inquired of Mr. Blackburn why he didn't represent himself in the proceeding. "Sam," he replied, quoting an old adage, "any lawyer who represents himself in a case has a fool for a client."

In 1926, J. B. Blackburn was selected as a juror in a criminal jury trial involving a man charged with stealing a hog. One woman made a particularly good prosecution witness in the case. In rebuttal, the defense attorney called this woman's husband as his first witness and asked him the following questions: "Do you know this woman?"

The man answered, "Yes, she's my wife."

"What is her general reputation for truth in the community?"

The man answered, "It is bad."

"Would you believe her under oath?"

[15]Mobile County Bar Association, *Stories of the Mobile Bar* (Mobile, AL: Mobile County Bar Association, 1983), p. 55.

The man answered, "No."

After the conclusion of the testimony and closing statements, one of the jurors stated to J. B. Blackburn as they were retiring to the jury room, "I'm not too worried about punishing the hog thief, but the man who testified against his wife ought to be hung!"

John E. Chason

John E. Chason

John Chason was born in Chatom, Alabama, on August 6, 1904. He graduated from the University of Alabama School of Law in 1928. When he was eight years old, Mr. Frank S. Stone, who was circuit solicitor, gave him his first pair of boxing gloves on the steps of the Washington County courthouse. John Chason would later become partners with Frank Stone's son, Norborne, Sr., then later Frank Stone's grandson, Norborne, Jr.

Mr. Chason had one client who purchased a barn with its contents and fixtures at a foreclosure sale. The debtor, who had lost the barn through foreclosure, pulled some rails and rope out of the barn subsequent to the sale, and Mr. Chason's client signed a warrant against the debtor for grand larceny and trespass. John Chason was to serve as special prosecutor in the case. By a quirk of fate John Chason did not walk to the courthouse on the trial date with his client. The debtor met Mr. Chason's client at the courthouse steps and shot him to death with a pistol. As the sheriff apprehended the debtor, the man remarked that he regretted that "he didn't get that lawyer Chason too," with the other bullets in his gun.

John Chason was once representing a criminal defendant who was alleged to have held up a store. He was cross-examining the store owner about the color of the hold-up man's clothes in an attempt to show the store owner's lack of memory about the event. He continued to ask the man about the color of each item of clothing the hold-up man was wearing at the time of the commission of the offense, getting the witness to admit he didn't remember the color of a particular item. When he asked, "Do you remember the color of the man's socks?" the exasperated witness answered, "Listen, sir, I don't know the color of any of those clothes because that man right there [pointing to Mr. Chason's client] had a big gun with a big barrel pointed right in my nose and I was so scared I wasn't looking at the color of his clothes!"

Louis Wesley Brannan

Louis Brannan

Louis Wesley Brannan graduated from the University of Alabama School of Law in 1928. He practiced law briefly in 1931 before beginning a career in business and politics. He served as mayor of Foley and spent twenty-four years in the Alabama House of Representatives and four years in the Alabama State Senate. In his words, he found the House of Representatives "like a boiler room full of whoopin' and hollerin' " in comparison to the Senate. He was instrumental in obtaining the separate Twenty-Eighth Judicial Circuit for Baldwin County in 1948. Mr. Brannan, who lived in Baldwin County from 1931 until his death, told me the following story illustrating his love for this county:

> There is one place in the Atlantic where a fresh water stream runs a great distance out into the ocean. One young ship captain who was desperately searching for fresh water after weeks of sailing, questioned his crew about where fresh water could be found. An old crewmate who knew of the existence of the fresh water stream told the captain, "Throw your bucket over the side right here." This is what I tell people passing through Baldwin County in search of a nice place to live—to throw their bucket over right here in Baldwin County."

Elliott Garrow Rickarby, Jr.

Elliott G. Rickarby, Jr.

Elliot Garrow Rickarby, Jr., was born on December 17, 1905. He graduated from the University of Mississippi and graduated from the University of Alabama School of Law with J. B. Blackburn, Louis Brannan and John Chason in the Class of 1928. He practiced for most of his career in Fairhope and died on April 18, 1976.

One story involved a contract for the sale of a car dealership prepared by Mr. Rickarby. At closing, the buyer read through the contract and said, "I don't understand anything that is going on here."

Mr. Rickarby looked at him and said, "I am Elliot Rickarby, a lawyer, this is a contract [handing him the contract], you are buying this car dealership, and [pointing to the seller] he is selling the car dealership. Now, sign this thing and let me get back to work!"

On another occasion, Mr. Rickarby was sitting in the courtroom while his junior partner, Dan Benton, was trying a difficult murder case. Dan Benton's client had taken the stand and had been caught in several lies while being cross-examined by the prosecutor.

During cross-examination, the defendant essentially admitted to being paid off to commit the murder. When he made this statement, Mr. Rickarby said in a loud voice, which was overheard by many people in the courtroom, "I guess the stock in Alabama Power Company is going to go up because this jury is about to send that man to the electric chair."

John Beebe

John Beebe

John Beebe was the second lawyer to practice law in Robertsdale, Alabama. He was born on February 9, 1899, and died on February 28, 1981.

Telfair James Mashburn, Jr.

Telfair James Mashburn, Jr., was born on August 22, 1907, in Flomaton, Alabama. He received his LLB from the University of Alabama in 1936. He began his practice in Bay Minette in 1941 and served in the United States Navy in World War II. He was elected the first judge of the Twenty-Eighth Judicial Circuit in 1948 and served from January 1949 through January 1953. He served in the Alabama House of Representatives from December 1962 through November 1964. He again served as circuit judge of the 28th Circuit from November 1964 through January 1977.

Telfair J. Mashburn, Jr.

Judge Mashburn tried one murder case after which the defendant was sentenced to the electric chair. He asked the defendant whether or not he had anything to say for himself before the sentence of law was pronounced. The defendant stated, "Yes, sir, Your Honor, I have. First, I'd like to thank you for the fair trial you give me. Second, I'd like to thank that there District Attorney for being fair to me and conducting himself right and proper. Third, I'd like to thank the prosecuting witnesses—I realize they did what they had to do. Fourth, I'd like to thank these here two defense lawyers you appointed to represent me. They did the best they could with what they had. Finally, I wanna say to them people in that jury box [as he angrily turned toward the jury box] Y'all done tore your pants with me!"

While Judge Mashburn was on the bench, he had a domestic case involving a husband and a wife. The husband would get drunk almost every night and come home and beat up his wife. She brought him to court before Judge Mashburn on a number of occasions and finally she solved her own problem. Judge Mashburn was pleased to discover that the wife was not having problems with the husband beating her any more and he asked her how she solved this problem. She mentioned that one night when he came in drunk, he got ready to beat her up, and she said to him, "You can go ahead and beat me up but I want you to remember one thing. You will have to go to sleep sometime, and when you do I am going to kill you." The husband never beat her again.

Orvis M. Brown

Orvis M. Brown, who was the first attorney to practice in Robertsdale, was born April 23, 1910, in Wilmer, Alabama, and died February 1, 1967. He received his LLB degree from the University of Alabama in 1934. Following his graduation he began his law practice in Robertsdale in September 1934 and practiced until 1942

Orvis M. Brown

C. Lenoir Thompson

C. Lenoir Thompson graduated from Jones Law School in 1937. He was admitted to the bar in 1937, and the first case he tried was a murder case in which he was appointed to represent the defendant. He was able to "save the man's hide" in spite of his inexperience.

Mr. Thompson was heavily involved in politics throughout his career and was involved in a number of campaigns. In one campaign, he was running against a politician who was the incumbent. Mr. Thompson was unable to attend one rally in Gateswood and sent his wife in his place. The incumbent spoke first and spoke at great length about all the wonderful things he had done for Baldwin County. After listening to the long-winded speech, Mrs. Thompson stood up and said, "It sounds to me like he takes credit for everything in Baldwin County except my son!"

C. Lenoir Thompson

For many years, all the lawyers in the county attended the opening of jury terms. Lenoir Thompson always wore a hat to court, and the presiding circuit judge drew names out of his hat to select the grand jury for service.

One of Fred Granade's first cases involved representing a woman in a divorce proceeding. Lenoir Thompson represented her husband. A portion of the cross-examination of the woman went as follows:

Mr. Thompson: "Don't you go down to the Silver Dollar bar every night without your husband and drink whiskey?"
Mr. Granade: "I object, your Honor."
Mr. Thompson: "It's true, Your Honor, I've seen her going in there with my own eyes!"

Lenoir Thompson once filed a petition for an annulment of a marriage which was shown to me by a local circuit judge. The petition read in part, "Comes now the Petitioner and requests this court to annul her marriage and as grounds for the petition states that the respondent [her husband] got drunk at their wedding reception and went home with his mama."

Throughout his years in law practice, Lenoir Thompson helped many of Baldwin County's poorer citizens who were unable to pay him adequately for his legal services.

Before entering practice, Lenoir worked for the State of Alabama. On one occasion, his assignment was to escort First Lady Eleanor Roosevelt to a reception in Montgomery. She arrived late and he angrily left the reception. Mr. Thompson kept a photograph in his office until his death which showed him walking out of the reception on Mrs. Roosevelt.

Mary T. White Richardson

Mary T. White Richardson was the first woman to practice law in Baldwin County. She was Lenoir Thompson's younger sister. She helped encourage Phyllis Nesbit in the early years of her practice as a woman lawyer in Baldwin County. Later in her life, she moved her law practice to Mobile.

Kenneth Cooper

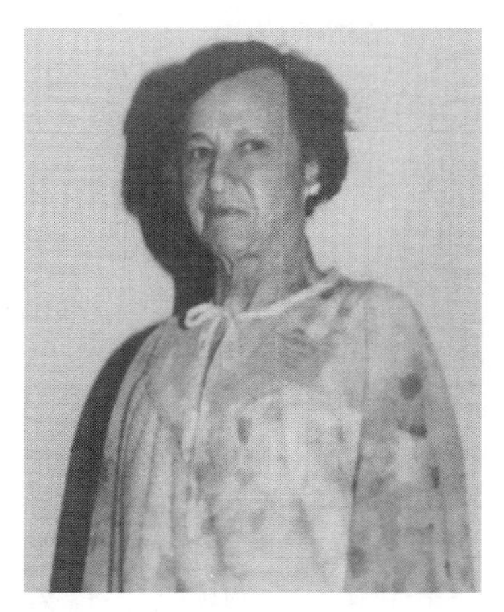

Mary T. White Richardson

Kenneth Cooper

Kenneth Cooper graduated from the University of Alabama in law in 1940. He served as the first District Attorney of the Twenty-Eighth Judicial Circuit. He was a retired lieutenant colonel in the U.S. Army Reserve and was very active in community charitable work during his tenure in practice in Bay Minette.

Forest A. Christian

Forest A. Christian

Forest A. Christian was born in Glasgow, Montana, and received his law degree from Southern Methodist University in Dallas. Upon graduation, he worked for the United States Department of Agriculture in Washington, D.C. He practiced in Foley, Alabama, from November 1, 1944, to December 31, 1976. It is interesting to note why Mr. and Mrs. Forest Christian moved to Foley, Alabama. One autumn day, they found a piece of cardboard with the word "Foley" printed on it while walking down Perry Street in Montgomery. They decided this was a good omen and they moved to Foley a few months later to find their fortune.

Cecil A. Chason

Cecil A. Chason

Cecil A. Chason graduated in 1940 from the University of Alabama School of Law and served as City Attorney for Foley for over thirty-five years.

Mr. Chason told me that shortly after he started practicing law, he was defending a non-jury case filed by Forest Christian. The suit was against a man who had signed the face of a promissory note without indicating whether or not he was endorsing the note or signing as a witness to the signature of the maker.

The case was set for late Friday afternoon before a judge who was "always ready to leave by noon on Friday." The judge called Mr. Chason into his chambers and said, "Cecil, I have reviewed this file carefully and I am afraid I will have to rule against you."

About ten minutes later, Mr. Christian approached Mr. Chason and asked if the case could be settled for any amount. Mr. Chason indicated it could not, because his client didn't have any money.

Mr. Christian then stated, "Cecil, I guess I will have to consent to a judgment in your favor. The judge just called me in and told me that he had carefully reviewed the file and he was afraid he would have to rule against me."

Norborne Clarke Stone, Jr.

Norborne C. Stone, Jr.

Norborne Clarke Stone, Jr., graduated from the University of Alabama in law in 1947. In 1983 he served as president of the Alabama Bar Association. He was selected as a Fellow in the American College of Trial Lawyers.

Mr. Stone once represented some local farmers in a case involving the application of a chemical to weeds on adjoining land. During application, the chemical drifted into Mr. Stone's client's pasture and killed some of his cows. Mr. Stone told his client to bring the drum the chemical was in when it was purchased to court with him on the day of trial. The farmer placed the drum in the trunk of his car on the unseasonably warm day of the trial. He brought the drum out of the hot weather into the air conditioned courtroom. After the farmer's testimony on direct examination, the drum was placed up near the jury box. A Mobile lawyer from an insurance defense firm was cross-examining the farmer about the chemical and making light of its mild effects and how this particular chemical could not have killed the cows in question. About that time, there was a tremendous boom in the courtroom and the lid blew off the chemical drum due to its being moved from the hot car to the cool courtroom. The jury literally left their seats with fright from the noise and the Mobile attorney jumped back and almost fainted. After this helpful experience, the jury went on to give a substantial award to Mr. Stone's client for the loss of his cattle.

James R. Owen

James R. Owen

James R. Owen was born in Bay Minette, Alabama, on March 11, 1922. He graduated from the University of Alabama School of Law in 1950 and began in private practice with J. B. Blackburn. He served in the Korean War from 1950 through 1952 and subsequently went back into practice in Bay Minette. He is a retired brigadier general in the Alabama National Guard.

Jimmy Owen was involved in a case in which his client was a waitress at a bar in Gulf Shores. She had a claim against an insurance company and while Mr. Owen was striking the jury, she mentioned to him that there was one regular customer of her bar that he should leave on the jury if possible. He was able to leave this man on the jury and as the jury walked past the counsel table to take their seats in the jury box, this man walked right up to Mr. Owen's client and gave her the "O.K." sign before taking his seat in the box. The attorney who represented the other party promptly buried his head in his hands when he saw the gesture.

James A. Hendrix

James A. Hendrix

James A. Hendrix served as District Attorney of Baldwin County for 26 years. He graduated from the University of Alabama School of Law in 1951.

I once showed a legal description with an imprecise beginning point to a local attorney who is a contemporary of Jim Hendrix. He mentioned that the most obscure beginning point he had encountered was contained in an old deed with a metes and bounds legal description that began, "Commencing at a point where my cow now stands..."

J. Connor Owens, Jr.

J. Connor Owens, Jr., was born in Roanoke, Alabama, December 20, 1923. He graduated from the University of Georgia School of Law in 1950 and was admitted to the Alabama Bar in 1951. He subsequently began his practice in Bay Minette.

J. Connor Owens, Jr.

Connor Owens told me a story about a case he tried in Mobile. He had a poor plaintiff's case that was going even worse than expected. The other lawyer was cross-examining Mr. Owens' client and elicited an answer that was detrimental to Mr. Owens' case. After this answer, the other party jumped up from the counsel table and made an obscene gesture to Mr. Owens' client. This gesture was seen by the entire jury and led to the case being settled by Mr. Owens for twice as much money as it was worth.

Ernest M. Bailey

Ernest M. Bailey

Ernest M. Bailey was born in 1917. He graduated from the University of Alabama in 1939 and University of Alabama School of Law in 1951. Mr. Bailey bought a farm to go into the egg business rather than a full-time law practice in Fairhope, but changed his mind after a short period in Fairhope. He practiced law in Fairhope for many years and served as a mentor for younger Eastern Shore attorneys.

A. Wilson Hayes

A. Wilson Hayes

Former circuit judge A. Wilson Hayes graduated in law from the University of Alabama in 1952.

He once told me a story about the first suit he tried as a lawyer before a local justice of the peace. Wilson Hayes' client was suing to collect a properly prepared, properly executed, and properly acknowledged promissory note that was signed by a local deadbeat. The deadbeat was unrepresented at the trial but the justice of the peace ruled in the local deadbeat's favor holding that "anyone crazy enough to lend money to him ought to lose it."

Tolbert M. Brantley

Tolbert Brantley

Tolbert M. Brantley was born in 1918 and graduated from the University of Alabama School of Law in 1949.

He and Harry J. Wilters, Jr., once represented a young, tall blond boy who was charged with assaulting a police officer. As Mr. Brantley was cross-examining the only eyewitness to the incident, they realized that he had very poor vision, and they believed he was lying about the identification of the man involved in the incident. Harry Wilters took over the cross-examination of the eyewitness and Tolbert Brantley slid his notepad and pen over in front of his client and hung his head. Mr. Wilters asked the identifying witness to stand up and point to the man who struck the police officer and he stood up and pointed directly at Tolbert Brantley.

In another case, Tolbert Brantley was representing a plaintiff who was severely injured in an automobile accident. Mr. Brantley demanded a jury trial. After the jury was impaneled, Mr. Brantley realized that one of his uncles was on the jury. The defendant did not show up at trial and Mr. Brantley offered proof of $20,000 in compensatory damages due to the plaintiff. The jury entered a verdict of $2,500 after hours of deliberation. Mr. Brantley asked a juror how they reached this decision. The juror said, "Your uncle would only let us give you $2,500 because he said he knew the defendant and knew that was all he could possibly pay."

Mobile County Courthouse circa 1900

Court Stories: Laughs From Across The Bay

M. A. "Bubba" Marsal was a well-known Mobile attorney who tried many cases in Baldwin County. During one case in Mobile, he was in the process of selecting a jury in a suit for monetary damages filed by his client. The New York lawyer defending the case had been sent to Mobile for the trial in question.

While qualifying the jury, the judge asked if any member of the jury panel was a friend of either lawyer. Five jurors stood up and responded that they were friends of Bubba Marsal. The New York lawyer turned to Bubba and said, "You certainly have a lot of friends!"

Bubba replied, "My real friends on that jury panel don't answer that particular question."

The story goes that this case was settled for a substantial sum shortly after this exchange between the lawyers.

~

As a young boy, Bubba loved to go to the courthouse in Mobile and watch the local lawyers try cases. He told me that in his opinion in those days Mr. Twitty was one of the best trial lawyers in the area.

Mr. Twitty once defended a civil case in which his client was sued for reportedly causing an accident at the corner of Government and Broad streets in Mobile.

The plaintiff was represented by a very dramatic lawyer who had few facts to support his case and was trying to sway the jury with a moving closing argument.

In a part of his closing argument, the plaintiff's lawyer said, "I have traveled all over the world. I have seen the pyramids in Egypt and the Eiffel Tower and many things in my life, but I have never seen a clearer case in which money should be awarded to my client."

In his response, Mr. Twitty replied, "This other lawyer here certainly took us all on a wonderful trip. He took us to the pyramids in Egypt, and he took us to the Eiffel Tower in Paris. But, I guess you noticed the only place he did not take us was to the corner of Government and Broad Street where this accident occurred in the first place!"

~

Bob Sherling worked for Bubba Marsal when he first began in law practice. Bubba Marsal had an ability to improvise and follow his instincts in the courtroom and still be very successful. No matter how complicated the case, Bubba would ask Bob to simplify the whole case and give him a one-page summary on their way to trial. Prior to trying one particularly complicated case, Bob went to great pains to condense everything to a one-page summary as instructed by Bubba. He handed Bubba the one-page summary on the morning of the trial, and Bubba looked at it and said, "Bob, I don't want to read all of that. Just tell me what happened."

~

Because Bubba was a gifted trial lawyer, he often took in more cases than anyone could humanly try in a law practice. I am told that in one of these cases, Bubba, representing the plaintiff, stood up and made a long, very eloquent opening statement. The defense counsel stood up after Bubba finished his remarks and said, "Ladies and gentlemen of the jury, that was one of the most eloquent opening statements I have heard given in any case. The problem with it is that it has nothing to do with this case!"

~

In one divorce case, Bubba represented the husband. Bubba believed the wife had been unfaithful to the husband, but was unable to prove the infidelity.

During his cross-examination, he asked the wife what she had been doing at another man's house and the testimony was that she had been at his house "making gravy."

Bubba argued throughout the rest of the trial that the lady ought to be punished for being out "making gravy" with other men rather than being home with her husband.

~

Tony Marsal contributed the following two stories.

> My father, Bubba, loved to shoot doves, and his friend, Judge Robert Irvin of Mobile, was also an avid dove hunter. One afternoon Judge Irvin was in the courtroom with a jury seated in the jury box. He was about to begin a criminal trial when Bubba came in the courtroom door and walked straight up to the bench. During the sidebar conference, Bubba told Judge Irvin there was a terrific dove field that was going to be shot that afternoon. As soon as the Assistant District Attorney began his opening statement in the case, Judge Irvin stopped him in the

middle of his first remarks and said, "What did you say! I am going to declare a mistrial." The Judge then hustled out of court, met Bubba in the hall and went to the dove shoot.

~

My father, Bubba, and I were late for one particular docket call before Judge Harry Wilters in the Baldwin County Circuit Court. As soon as Bubba got there, Judge Wilters angrily said, "Bubba, I am going to find you in contempt of court for being late and fine you fifty dollars."

Bubba walked to the bench and said, "Judge, all I have got is a hundred-dollar bill. Do you have change?" The entire courtroom howled with laughter over Bubba's remark.

~

The following five stories are reprinted with the permission of the Mobile County Bar Association from a pamphlet entitled *Stories of the Mobile Bar,* copyright 1983. This pamphlet is available through the Mobile County Bar Association.

~

Mr. Harry Seale contributed the following story to the pamphlet:

> Ben Turner represented J. B. Burford, a Choctaw County man, who was charged with transporting cattle across the state line without a permit and without the cattle being inoculated. Turner proved to the jury that Mr. Burford had an enormous pasture, part of which was in Alabama and part in Mississippi. He always put the fresh, newly purchased cattle on the Alabama side of the pasture, but the Mississippi side was covered with bounteous, green, succulent grass, and the cattle naturally strolled over where the grass was greenest. Mr. Burford would then withdraw the cattle from the pasture on the Mississippi side and transport them to Waynesboro, Mississippi, for shipment to various packing houses. Mr. Turner

convinced the jurors that Mr. Burford had not transported the cattle, but they themselves had walked over into Mississippi, and the jury promptly acquitted Mr. Burford.

~

Mr. Thomas A. Hamilton wrote the following regarding a Baldwin County case:

Many years ago, I was representing a small bank in Baldwin County in a suit in Bay Minette on a guaranty of a promissory note. The defendant was the brother of the sheriff of Baldwin County, who, as such, had powerful influence over the citizenry…

My principal witness was the bank's president, and on cross-examination Mr. Robert E. Gordon, attorney for the defendant, pounced on the witness with the common trick question, "Whom have you talked with about this case?"…

The bank president, being a very honest man, said "I talked with Mr. Hamilton about it."

Mr. Gordon asked, "When?" and the witness replied, "Just before the trial started."

Mr. Gordon then asked, "What did you tell Mr. Hamilton about this case?"

I rose to object that the question called for privileged, confidential communications, but, before I could complete my objection, the witness blurted out, "I told Mr. Hamilton we were going to have a heck of a time winning this case."

That did it. Judge Hare nearly fell over backwards, and the jury was convulsed.

Needless to say, I lost the case.

~

Mr. Hamilton also shared the following tale:

Judge Tisdale J. Touart, of the Inferior Court, was hearing a case wherein several defendants were charged with participation in an affray, with Harry Seale as defense counsel. In the course of the hearing one of the defendants was on the witness stand, and the judge, as was his wont, questioned her. The judge asked, "Miss, were you cut in the fracas?" She rolled her eyes and replied, "No, Judge, I wasn't cut in the fracas. I was cut in the stomach, midway 'twixt the naval and the fracas."

~

The next story was shared by the late Walter M. Cook:

My introduction to the practice in the late 1940s was to assist Dan Thomas from time to time in insignificant matters which he wished to escape. Later, Dan ascended to the office of U.S. District Judge. However, during the interim, I recall one principle which was firmly impressed upon me (as related to Dan).

The firm represented a railroad from time to time called upon to defend itself for the killing of a farmer's cow. Always at the time of the accident, according to the farmer, the cow was a prized animal; and the railroad always actively defended each case....

The principle referred to, which, although well known, [is] but seldom followed among trial lawyers, is... "Examine well the witness, but do not ask an unnecessary question, just for the sake of having the last word."

Well, Dan was trying the typical railroad case on a hot summer day in which the farmer was not reluctant to testify as to the enormous value of his "prize cow" which the railroad had "run upon or against, and killed." Dan proved that the train was coming around a curve, things were going well for him, and he had the flagman on the stand who dutifully testified that when he saw the half-starved animal on the track, he called out a warning to the engineer.

And then Dan made the fatal mistake of asking one more question, i.e., "What did the engineer say?"...which elicited the following response:

"He said—WATCH ME HIT THAT S.O.B.!!"

Thus ended the case.

Justice Douglas Inge Johnstone shared the following about Herndon Inge, Jr.'s first criminal case. Justice Johnstone refers to Mr. Inge by his nickname "Wank" in the story:

> Wank's client, who ran a filling station, was accused of selling beer on Sunday. His story was that on a Saturday his customer bought a case of beer but asked whether he could leave it in the clients' icehouse until the next day, Sunday, when the customer would pick it up on his way to meet his fishing buddies. The customer explained that his wife didn't allow him to have beer at home.
>
> Wank did legal research on the question of when title passes in a sale of goods and wrote Judge Wilson an elaborate brief of both the law and the facts. At the trial, Wank argued passionately that the sale had been consummated on Saturday when the customer paid for the beer and first laid hands on it—that the next day, the Sunday in question, Wank's client was a mere gratuitous bailee holding the beer for its new owner.
>
> Judge Wilson looked kindly on the young lawyer and, at the end of the arguments, said, "Mr. Inge, your sincerity and the care with which you have presented the law and the facts convince me that your client is not guilty, and I find him not guilty."
>
> As Wank, elated with victory, reached the sidewalk, his client slapped him on the back and said, "Gosh, thanks, Mr. Inge: You know, if I couldn't sell beer on Sunday, I'd go stone broke."

Court Stories: More Tales

My wife's grandfather, Justice Robert T. Simpson, who was an Alabama Supreme Court justice, referred to Saturday as "If-A-Man Day." According to him, many clients think that if they can catch a lawyer in his or her office on Saturday, they can obtain free legal advice. They usually begin their request for such advice by stating "*If a man* were to...," hence the name "If-A-Man Day."

Fairhope attorney Richard Lacey shared the following story, which occurred during his early years in practice.

> Attorneys John Chason and Cecil Chason were brothers. They started a shouting match in court while representing their respective clients in a hotly contested case. Their mother happened to be in the courtroom and she got so embarrassed by their fussing that she stood up in court and made them stop.

~

Attorney John Duck in Fairhope once filed an action to collect an open account against a man being defended by Elliot Rickarby, Jr. At trial the man who owed the account ruined his own case with his answers to Mr. Rickarby's questions. After the trial, Mr. Rickarby angrily asked his client, "Why didn't you answer the questions the way you did in my office yesterday?"

To which the man replied, "I wasn't under oath in your office!"

~

Due to space limitations, I was only able to include photographs in this chapter of lawyers beginning their practice in Baldwin County in 1952 or earlier.

8

History: Twenty-Eighth Judicial Circuit

Circuit Judges of the 28th Judicial Circuit and Their Periods of Service

Telfair J. Mashburn, Jr. (1949–1953) (1964–1977)
Hubert Hall (1953–1964)
A. Wilson Hayes (1977–1982)
Harry J. Wilters, Jr. (1975–1989)
Floyd C. Enfinger, Jr. (1982–1985)
Thomas B. Norton, Jr. (1984–1993)
Charles C. Partin III (1985–present)
James H. Reid (1989–present)
Pamela Baschab (1993–1997)—currently serving on the Alabama Court of Criminal Appeals
Lyn S. Stuart (1997–2001)—currently serving on the Supreme Court of Alabama
Robert Wilters (1999–present)
J. Langford Floyd (2001–present)

Telfair J. Mashburn, Jr.

Hubert Hall

A. Wilson Hayes

Harry J. Wilters, Jr.

Floyd C. Enfinger, Jr.

Thomas B. Norton, Jr.

Charles C. Partin III

James H. Reid

Pamela Baschab

Lyn S. Stuart

Robert Wilters

J. Langford Floyd

District Judges of the 28th Judicial Circuit and Their Periods of Service

Arthur Epperson (1977–1989)
Phyllis S. Nesbit (1977–1989)
Pamela Baschab (1989–1993)
Lyn S. Stuart (1989–1997)
Robert Wilters (1993–1999)
Rosalyn Mattingly (1999–2001)
Narissa G. Nelson (2001–present)
Jody Bishop (2001–present)
J. Langford Floyd (1997–2000)
Carmen Bosch (elected June 25, 2002, to take office in January 2003)

Arthur Epperson

Phyllis S. Nesbit

Pamela Baschab

Lyn S. Stuart

Robert Wilters

Rosalyn Mattingly

Narissa Nelson

Jody Bishop

J. Langford Floyd

Carmen Bosch

District Attorneys of the 28th Judicial Circuit and Their Periods of Service

Kenneth Cooper (1947–1951)
William Lauten (1951–1953)
Kenneth Cooper (1953–1955)
James A. Hendrix (1955–January 1981)
Thomas B. Norton, Jr. (January 1981–October 1984)
David Whetstone (October 1984–present)

Kenneth Cooper

William Lauten

James A. Hendrix

Thomas B. Norton, Jr.

David Whetstone

Judges of Probate of the 28th Judicial Circuit and Their Periods of Service

W. R. Stuart (1944–1963)
L. D. Owen, Jr. (1963–1965)
Harry D'Olive, Sr. (1965–1993)
Harry D'Olive, Jr. (1993–1995)
Adrian Johns (1995–to present)

W. R. Stuart

L. D. Owen, Jr.

Harry D'Olive, Sr.

Harry D'Olive, Jr.

Adrian T. Johns

Sheriffs of the 28th Judicial Circuit and Their Periods of Service

Taylor Wilkins, Sr. (1946–1975)
Thomas H. Benton (1975–1986)
James B. Johnson (1986–present)

Taylor Wilkins, Sr.

Thomas H. Benton

James B. Johnson

Baldwin County Law Enforcement Memorial

Clerks and Register of the 28th Judicial Circuit and Their Periods of Service

Alice Duck (November 1946–1971), Clerk
Eunice Blackmon (1971–1989), Clerk
Jackie Calhoun (1989–present), Clerk
Eunice Tindal (1971–1990), Register

Alice Duck

Eunice Blackmon

Jackie Calhoun

Eunice Tindal

Court Stories: More Tales

Mr. Charles Bodden of Bay Minette told me this story about attorney Norborne C. Stone, Sr., who practiced law in Bay Minette from 1917 until his death at the age of 31 years. Mr. Stone was employed to collect some money from a North Baldwin County man who had a reputation for being violent and dangerous. He had written the man a collection letter with no results, and Mr. Stone's client was in his office urging him to hurry up and collect the money. The client leaned across Mr. Stone's desk, with his finger pointed at Mr. Stone, and loudly stated, "I hired you to collect that money, now hurry up and get it done! You shouldn't be afraid of the man!"

Mr. Stone replied, "Sir, we need to proceed very carefully; that man is dangerous and might..."

At that moment the client looked out the window and saw the violent man headed toward Mr. Stone's office. The shocked client jumped up and hurried to the door stating, "I've got to leave right now, but don't you forget to hurry up and collect that money!"

~

Mamie White of Bay Minette contributed a story about some expensive Baldwin County goat meat "purchased" in 1939. During that year two local men were arrested while butchering a goat they had stolen from a local farm. They were later convicted of larceny and received a heavy fine which made their goat meat some of the most costly in Baldwin County history.

~

Jim Curenton of Fairhope, who once represented a logger who filed a lawsuit against one of Dan Blackburn's clients, sent this story to me:

> We were in Dan Blackburn's office in Bay Minette taking my client's deposition, along with two other attorneys from out of town. As usual, Mr. Blackburn was doing an excellent job in examining my client, and at one point, Mr. Blackburn questioned my client as follows:

Blackburn: Now, Mr. P— would you tell me if you have ever been convicted of a felony?

Mr. P—: Well, yes I have.

Blackburn: (*Beginning to smile and eyes beginning to light up*) You have? Well, would you tell me what was the felony?

Mr. P—: (*In all sincerity*) It was alimony.

Blackburn: (*Looking confused*) I don't understand. Could you please explain?

Mr. P—: Well, you're the lawyer. Why don't you explain it to me?

All in the room chuckled while Dan moved on to the next line of questions. Later I learned through hearsay that Mr. P— had failed to pay his alimony as ordered, and the sheriff's deputies were sent out to arrest him pursuant to a court order. They found Mr. P— at the local dirt race track driving a water truck around the oval, watering down the dust. The deputies, not knowing what he looked like, approached the water truck and asked where they could find Mr. P—. My client then told them that the last time he saw Mr. P—, he was standing up beside the concession stand ordering a beer. The deputies thanked Mr. P— for telling them where they could find their suspect and immediately proceeded up the side of the hill toward the stand. Mr. P— then drove the water truck out the gate and to his home in the northwest Florida woods. Later the deputies discovered they had been duped and successfully located Mr. P—, whereupon he was arrested. Mr. P— was brought to court and, indeed was convicted of some conduct relating to his failure to pay alimony and relating to the information he gave the deputies.

~

Several years ago, we had what I will call a vision-challenged client who telephoned our Daphne office to speak with "her lawyer." Our receptionist asked her which lawyer, of the eight lawyers in our firm, was her lawyer.

She responded, "I don't know his name, but I remember he is good looking." After first trying several other lawyers in our firm, the receptionist buzzed me and said, "Mr. Crosby, there is a lady on the phone who can't remember which lawyer she talked with, but she said he was good looking."

I replied, "You know it is not me. Try all the other lawyers in the law firm."

After trying the rest of the lawyers, the receptionist buzzed me again and said, "They say it's not them. What shall I do?"

I responded, "Let me speak with this lady."

I picked up the phone and answered, "This is Sam Crosby, can I help you?"

She said, "Are you my lawyer?"

I replied, "No, I can't be your lawyer if he is good looking."

She said, "Yes, you are; I recognize your voice!"

I could hear our receptionist giggling as I replied, "Ma'am, when was the last time you visited your optometrist?"

~

Marion "Tut" Wynne of Fairhope told me of a story involving a civil case in which the woman who brought the case claimed that her right arm was seriously injured in a car wreck.

During her direct examination by her lawyer, she testified that, as a result of the car accident, she could no longer lift her right arm above her waist.

On cross-examination the defense counsel gambled and asked, "Would you please show the members of the jury how high you could raise your right arm before this car wreck?" Whereupon the lady raised her right arm over her head.

~

Fairhope resident Rick Boone shared the following story regarding the "defense of a goat" by Norborne Stone, Jr.

Rick's father, Lester Boone, lived on Church Street and had a pet goat named "Mugsy." The goat was beloved by the neighborhood children. One night two dogs came into the yard and tried to attack Mugsy, and Lester discharged a shotgun to scare the dogs off. The city charged Mr. Boone with the violation of a municipal ordinance for keeping an unlawful goat within the city limits.

Prior to the trial, it came to light that the mayor kept a horse in his backyard. By keeping the horse in his yard, the mayor was violating the same municipal ordinance. When Mr. Stone called this fact to prosecutor's attention, charges were dismissed, and Mr. Boone and Mugsy were free of the long arm of the law.

~

The following true account of two days of a local attorney's schedule gives an accurate picture of the general practice of law in Baldwin County, Alabama, in the year 1986. One day, the lawyer was at a Wall Street law office in New York City reviewing documents pertaining to the sale of Baldwin County real estate by one of the lawyer's clients. Two days later the same lawyer was defending a dog killing case in the District Court of Baldwin County.

~

In our profession, the amusing events occur faster than they can be recorded. In past years, different members of our firm have seen a woman who wanted to bequeath $30,000 to her dog, a man who wanted to open a "legal" house of ill repute, and a woman who had a parachutist land in her glass display at the Greater Gulf States Fair.

9

History: Some Baldwin County "Firsts"

Baldwin County has a history of leading the state in judicial and legal service by local women. Some examples include the following:

In 1974, Justice Janie Ledlow Shores, who is originally from Loxley, became the first woman ever to serve on the Supreme Court of Alabama. She was also the first woman to be popularly elected to a State Supreme Court in the nation.

Janie Ledlow Shores

In January, 2000, Justice Lyn Stuart became Baldwin County's second woman to serve on the Supreme Court of Alabama.

The first woman elected as a trial judge in the State of Alabama was Phyllis S. Nesbit, who assumed office on January 19, 1977.

The first woman to practice law in Baldwin County was Mary Thompson White Richardson.

On March 8, 2002, Ginny Granade became the first woman in history to serve as a federal district judge in the Southern District of the United States District Court. Ginny Granade was also the first woman Assistant U.S. Attorney for the Southern District from Baldwin County.

In August 1981, Greer Minic Wilhelm became the first woman Assistant District Attorney in Baldwin County history.

Mary E. Murchison and Margaret G. Thomas formed the first all-woman law firm in Baldwin County.

On August 5, 1999, Rosalyn Mattingly became the first African-American to serve as a District Judge for Baldwin County.

In January 1997, Pamela Baschab became the first Baldwin County lawyer to serve on the Alabama Court of Criminal Appeals.

Since the creation of Baldwin County's District Court in 1977, five of the nine judges who have served have been women.

Other Baldwin County "firsts" include the following:

Larry C. Moorer

Norborne C. Stone, Jr.

In February of 1984, Larry C. Moorer became the first African-American attorney to practice law in Baldwin County.

The first Baldwin County attorney to be selected for a jury venire was Kenneth Cooper.

In July, 1982, E. E. Ball became the first local attorney to serve on a jury.

In 1983, Norborne C. Stone, Jr., became the first Baldwin County attorney to serve as president of the Alabama State Bar Association.

Court Stories: More Tales

One story Norborne Stone, Jr. tells is about a federal court action that was filed against a private school in Mississippi by a student at the school who claimed his civil rights were being abridged by the school requirement of short haircuts. The headmaster of the school was being cross-examined by the boy's lawyer and the exchange went as follows:

Q Headmaster Jones, don't you realize that Thomas Jefferson and the other founding fathers of this country had long hair?

A Yes, I do, but none of them attended our private school!

~

At one court term Michael Zoghby, a circuit judge from Mobile, was about to appoint a lawyer to represent a defendant. The judge asked him, "Would you like for me to appoint a lawyer to represent you?"

The man responded, "No Judge, I don't think I'll need a lawyer. I plan on telling the truth."

~

Retired District Judge Arthur Epperson said he convicted a man of killing three doves over the legal limit shortly after beginning his tenure as a district judge. He fined the man $100 and the man irately said, "Judge, that sentence is unfair. The last *five* times I have been caught the fine was only $10 per bird over the limit. That has always been the fine here in Baldwin County."

~

Another old yarn involved a birddog named "Lawyer," who was the best birddog in Alabama. He would point, back the point of other dogs, and find quail anywhere you put him.

His owner had an acquaintance he took hunting with Lawyer, and Lawyer did a beautiful job. When they finished hunting the acquaintance said to Lawyer's owner, "I'll give you five thousand dollars for Lawyer."

Lawyer's owner said, "No deal."

The acquaintance said, "Name your price for Lawyer, I'll pay anything."

Lawyer's owner replied, "He's not for sale."

The next year the dog's owner was approached by the same acquaintance about buying Lawyer. "How much will you sell me Lawyer for?" said the acquaintance.

Lawyer's owner said, "How about five dollars?"

The acquaintance asked, "Why? I can't understand it—last year you wouldn't sell him for any amount."

The owner replied, "I loaned Lawyer to a friend, and they accidentally called him 'Judge' throughout a hunt, and he hasn't been worth a hoot since!"

~

Attorney Laurence McDuff of Birmingham recently tried a case in a rural Alabama county. The case illustrated how we lawyers often do not communicate our points very well in the courtroom. Laurence said he and opposing counsel spent much of the first trial day arguing about the meaning of a particular Alabama statute. At the end of the day a co-defendant, who had been in court all day, turned to Laurence and said, "Mr. McDuff, I didn't have any idea what you two were arguing about. I thought a statute was a naked man in concrete."

10

History: Local Bar Association, Bar Presidents, and Current Attorneys

Bay Minette Courthouse – 2001

Local Bar Association

Baldwin County's local bar association came into existence as an organization shortly after legislation was enacted on August 16, 1947, creating the new Twenty-Eighth Judicial Circuit. The new judicial circuit was a separate circuit which included only Baldwin County. Prior to creation of the new circuit, Baldwin County had been one of the four counties comprising the Twenty-First Judicial Circuit.

In the early 1940s all the attorneys who practiced in the Twenty-First Judicial Circuit began to meet once a year for a cookout. The location for the cookout was rotated among Baldwin, Conecuh, Escambia, and Monroe Counties, the four counties that composed the 21st Judicial Circuit.

With the advent of the 28th Judicial Circuit, the Baldwin County Bar Association had its own identity and began to have its own meetings. At an early meeting, John Chason was elected the first president of the Baldwin County Bar Association. In 1949, J. B. Blackburn was elected the first representative to the Alabama Board of Bar Commissioners. In 1967, Phyllis Nesbit served as the first woman president of the Baldwin County Bar Association.

The Association began meeting for its functions at the old Malbis Restaurant, which is no longer in existence, and later moved its annual meetings to Probate Judge Harry D'Olive's camp on Sibley Creek. As a result of his hospitality, in 1985 Judge D'Olive became the only non-lawyer ever given a lifetime membership in the bar association.

Some of the most colorful moments in the Bar Association's history occurred at annual cookouts at Judge D'Olive's camp. On one occasion, a local lawyer was showing off his new speedboat to the entire Bar Association. The lawyer was racing the boat along Sibley Creek, lost control of the boat, and ran it out on a bank and well back into the woods.

At another annual meeting, one lawyer took a wrong turn while walking through the woods to his car and would have spent the night in the swamp had Judge D'Olive not rescued him.

During its forty-year history, the Baldwin County Bar Association has evolved from primarily a social organization to a service organization that has endorsed numerous measures to improve our court system. The Association has also sponsored such programs as the historic Baldwin County term of the Alabama Supreme Court held on November 21, 1986, at Faulkner State Junior College. Nearly 2000 people attended this court session, which was coordinated and opened by local attorney Allan Chason. Area attorneys who presented arguments to the court were Robert Wills, Tolbert Brantley, Samuel Crosby, Daniel Blackburn, and Linda Perry.

Fairhope Courthouse – 2001

Bar Presidents

A list of the Baldwin County Bar Association presidents and their dates of service follows:[16]

John E. Chason	1947–1948
Jefferson J. Bennett	1949–1950
Norborne C. Stone, Jr.	1953–1954
James R. Owen	1957–1958
Harry J. Wilters, Jr.	Unknown
Tolbert M. Brantley, Jr.	Unknown
Forrest Christian	1963–1964
Kenneth Cooper	1964–1965
Phyllis S. Nesbit	1966–1967

[16]Compiled from the records of the Baldwin County Bar Association.

Cecil G. Chason	1967–1968
J. Connor Owens, Jr.	1968
Lloyd E. Taylor	1973–1974
E. E. Ball	1974–1975
Taylor Wilkins, Jr.	1975–1976
Charles C. Partin	1976–1977
Francis A. Poggi, Jr.	1977–1978
Daniel A. Benton	1978–1979
Claude E. Bankester	1979–1980
Ronald E. Kopesky	1980–1981
Julian B. Brackin	1981–1982
Robert A. Wills	1982–1983
Thomas W. Underwood, Jr.	1983–1984
James H. Reid, Jr.	1984–1985
Allan R. Chason	1985–1986
Marion E. Wynne, Jr.	1986–1987
Samuel N. Crosby	1987–1988
H. Young Dempsey	1988–1989
Charles C. Simpson	1989
Mollie P. Johnson	1989–1990
Mary E. Murchison	1990–1991
Fred K. Granade	1991–1992
David P. Shepherd	1992–1993
W. Donald Bolton, Jr.	1993–1994
John E. Chason	1994–1995
Larry P. Sutley	1995–1996
Gary L. Armstrong	1996–1997
David A. Simon	1997–1998
James H. Sweet	1998–1999
W. Beatty Pearson	1999–2000
Daniel G. Blackburn	2000–2001
Oliver Latour	2001–2002
James E. Smith	2002

Foley Courthouse – 2001

2002 List of Baldwin County Attorneys with Principal Office in Baldwin County

Alves, Shawn T.
Armstrong, Gary L.
Bailey, Andrew
Bagwell, David A.
Ball, E. E.
Bankester, Daniel T.
Bear, Thomas O.
Beck, John
Bellucci, Vincent A.
Bennett, Barry
Benton, Daniel A.
Biles, Bayless E.
Bishop, Hon. Jody
Blackburn, Daniel G.
Bolton, Joseph M., Jr.
Bolton, W. Donald, Jr.
Bosch, Carmen E.
Brackin, Julian B.
Brantley, William L.
Bruijn, Pascal
Byrd, William I. Hon.
Calhoun, William Daniel
Campbell, Elizabeth
Campbell, Jody W.
Carr, Charles F.
Carr, Jeff B.
Cater, R. Paul
Chandler, Walter B.
Chapman, G. David
Chason, Allan R.
Chason, John Earle
Chunn, L. Brian

Citrin, Andrew T.
Collins, Patrick B.
Conner, David
Corte, Cheryl Eubanks
Crabtree, Jeffrey W.
Craven, Daniel H.
Crosby, Samuel N.
Cummins, Manley L.
Curenton, James G.
Daniell, David
Daniels, Marie
Dasinger, Brian
Dasinger, Michael A. III
Dasinger, Thomas E.
Davenport, Tara
Davis, Richard E.
Davis, Spencer
Dawkins, Greg
Dixon, Hallie S.
Doerr, Donald D., Jr.
Dorgan, James
Drake, Naomi
Drummond, Robert D.
Enfinger, Floyd C., Jr.
Ferrell, Kathryn D.
Fields, Leslie T.
Fincher, Jim Clay
Floyd, Hon. J. Lang
Gaines, Rebecca A.
Gamble, John
Garner, Timothy D.
Gober, Mark
Gonas, John S.
Goolsby, Craig W.
Granade, Fred K.
Ham, Charles
Harrell, Andrew
Hart, Michelle M.
Hayes, Wilson
Heard, W. Kenneth
Henderson, Sarah
Hendrix, James A.
Herbert, Jule R.
Hicks, Preston L.
Hipsh, Larry H.
Hitson, Kenneth A.
Hoff, Richard N.
Hoiles, Sharon R.
Hollon, Frank Turner
Holt, Thaddeus
Howard, Linda
Hughes, Mark E.
Inge, Sam W.
Irby, Samuel W.
Isphording, Brian C.
Irvine, George R. III
Jensen, Richard
Johnson, Stephen P.
Jones, Lawrence
Jovings, Sam
Kemp, Karol
Klyce, Thomas W.
Koons, Harold A. III
Kopesky, Ronald E.
Lacey, Richard C.
Lassiter, Byron A.
Latour, Oliver J., Jr.
Leatherbury, Greg L., Jr.
Lee, Deidre White
Lewis, R. Scott
Lipscomb, J. Alan
Mantiply, Mallory
Mantiply, Mary Beth
Mashburn, Hon. Telfair J.
Matheny, David
Maumenee, Benjamin C.

May, James W.
May, Joyce K.
McDill, Jessica
McDuffie, Michael H.
McGlothren, Michael
McGriff, Kelly A.
McKerall, Samuel G.
McKinney, J. Randle
McMeans, Cynthia
McRae, C. Bennett
Meurer, Michelle
Middleton, Stephen, M.
Mikul, Leonard F.
Mitchell, Daniel P.
Monahan, B. Andrew
Moore, Gary A.
Moore, T. Deven
Morgan, Stanley
Morris, Charles H. III
Morris, Craig
Murchison, Mary E.
Myers, Wilson
Nelson, Hon. Narissa G.
Nesbit, Hon. Phyllis S.
Newcomb, Judy A.
Noletto, Van
Norton, C. Joseph
Norton, Thomas B., Jr.
Olmstead, Craig D.
Olmstead, Rosanne L.
Overstreet, Adam
Owen, James R.
Owen, L. D., III
Partin, Hon. Charles C.
Pearce, Allyson C.
Pearson, Steven Campbell
Pearson, W. Beatty
Perry, Lynn
Perry, Michelle
Pfeifer, William L., Jr.
Pierce, Wendy A.
Pigott, J. Russell "Rusty"
Pilcher, Mary E.
Pittman, James B., Jr.
Porter, Diane
Powell, James C.
Pritchett, Stephen
Pryor, Caroline T.
Raines, Kenneth R.
Rapp, Vincent G.
Reid, Hon. James H.
Rone, Matthew
Rucker, Meredith
Ryan, David A.
Ryan, Mark
Salmon, Michael
Salter, Stephen
Scroggins, James M.
Scully, William E., Jr.
Shepherd, David P.
Sherman, Cynthia J.
Simon, David A.
Simpson, Charles C. III
Sisson, William S.
Slade, Charles Kenneth
Smith, Harry C.
Smith, James D.
Smith, James E.
Stanard, Chandler
Stankoski, D. Robert
Stankoski, J. Clark
Stein, G. Barker, Jr.
Stone, Norborne C., Jr.
Stone, Sheila V.
Stuart, Hon. Lyn
Sullivan, Molly

Sutley, Larry P.
Swaim, M. Mort
Sweet, James H.
Taber, John
Taylor, Bert P.
Taylor, Helene H.
Taylor, Jeremy
Taylor, Lloyd E.
Taylor, Mary
Taylor, Scott P.
Terry, Steven L.
Thompson, B. J.
Underwood, Thomas W.
Upton, Mark
Vaughn, David P.
Vollmer, Jim
Waller, Tara S.
Watson, Russell
Wendt, Cali
Whetstone, J. David
Wilkins, Taylor D., Jr.
Williams, Thomas P.
Wills, Elizabeth S.
Wills, Robert A.
Wilters, Hon. Harry J., Jr.
Wilters, Hon. Robert
Winston, Norman
Wood, Patricia
Wyatt, J. Alex
Wynne, Marion E., Jr.
Yazdi, Habib
Zundel, Susan

Note: Please accept my apologies for any omissions or errors on this list. We tried to check the local bar listings and local phone books at the time this list was completed in order to be accurate.

Afterword

As long as we humans are actors in the court system, there will be an abundance of humor.

Included in this book are tales related to me by other lawyers from unknown sources. Please forgive me if I did not give appropriate attribution to any source. All errors and omissions in this book are strictly mine; please accept my apologies.

I thank you for taking your valuable time to read this book and I hope you have enjoyed it.

Most of all, I am thankful to my Heavenly Father, my Lord Jesus Christ, and the Holy Spirit for my faith, my health, my family, and for allowing me to live in this great county and serve its citizens as an officer of the court.

Index

Entries in **bold type** indicate pages containing photographs.